# Good Housekeeping

# Calorie Counter Cookbook

PAVILION

First published in the United Kingdom in 2014 by
Pavilion
1 Gower Street
London
WC1E 6HD

The Good Housekeeping website is

www.goodhousekeeping.co.uk

10 9 8 7 6 5 4 3 2 1

ISBN 978-1-909397-89-7

A catalogue record for this book is available from the British Library.

Reproduction by Mission Productions Ltd, Hong Kong

Printed and bound by Times Offset (M) Sdn Bhd, Malaysia

This book can be ordered direct from the publisher at www.pavilionbooks.com

## Picture Credits

Photographers:
Neil Barclay (page 21); Steve Baxter (pages 14, 53, 59, 104, 128, 131, 154, 166, 179, 180 and 184); Nicki Dowey (pages 16, 17, 19, 20, 22, 40, 46, 47, 49, 62, 69, 70, 72, 73, 76, 81, 83, 91, 100, 112, 134, 137, 138, 147, 153, 157, 158, 161, 162, 174, 185, 193 and 199); Will Heap (page 63); Diane Miller (page 182); Gareth Morgans (pages 2, 6, 24, 30, 42, 55, 60, 63, 77, 84, 87, 88, 94, 97, 101, 107, 111, 117, 119, 120, 127, 132, 140, 142, 143, 165, 169, 170, 176, 189, 190, 195 and 196); Myles New (pages 45, 78, 108, 125, 144 and 173); Ria Osbourne (page 74); Craig Robertson (pages 37, 50, 51 and 198); Maya Smend (page 34); Lucinda Symons (pages 148 and 150); Jon Whitaker (page 26, 56, 92, 102 and 122); Kate Whitaker (pages 29, 33, 39, 66, 98, 114 and 187).

Stylists:
Susannah Blake, Tamzin Ferdinando, Lisa Harrison, Cynthia Inions, Rachel Jukes, Penny Markham, Wei Tang, Sarah Tildesley, Helen Trent, Fanny Ward, Polly Webb-Wilson and Mari Mererid Williams.

Home Economists:
Meike Beck, Anna Burges-Lumsden, Monaz Dumasia, Joanna Farrow, Emma Jane Frost, Teresa Goldfinch, Alice Hart, Zoë Horne, Jenny Iggleden, Lucy McKelvie, Jennie Milsom, Kim Morphew, Aya Nishimura, Katie Rogers, Bridget Sargeson, Stella Sargeson, Sarah Tildesley, Kate Trend, Charlotte Watson, Jennifer White and Mari Mererid Williams.

## Notes

The values for unbranded foods have been obtained from McCance & Widdowson's *The Composition of Foods* (6th summary edition and subsequent supplements), and have been reproduced under the terms of the Open Government Licence. Those for branded items have been obtained from the websites of supermarkets and food manufacturers.

Both metric and imperial measures are given for the recipes. Follow either set of measures, not a mixture of both, as they are not interchangeable.
All spoon measures are level.
1 tsp = 5ml spoon; 1 tbsp = 15ml spoon.
Ovens and grills must be preheated to the specified temperature.
Medium eggs should be used except where otherwise specified.

## Dietary Guidelines

Note that certain recipes contain raw or lightly cooked eggs. The young, elderly, pregnant women and anyone with immune-deficiency disease should avoid these because of the slight risk of salmonella.
Note that some recipes contain alcohol. Check the ingredients list before serving to children.

# Contents

HOW TO USE THIS BOOK                6

RECIPES UNDER 300 CALORIES         14

RECIPES UNDER 400 CALORIES         78

RECIPES UNDER 500 CALORIES         144

A-Z CALORIE COUNTS                 200

INDEX                              238

# HOW TO USE THIS BOOK

# Calorie Counting Made Easy

**Whether you want to lose weight, maintain your weight or gain weight, this book will help you get more calorie savvy. You'll find ideas for recipes under 300, 400 and 500 calories, plus the calorie values of more than 1,200 popular foods and drinks, including staples, such as milk, bread and meat, as well as many branded products, takeaways and restaurant dishes.**

Calorie counting may sound old hat, but any nutritionist will tell you that when it comes to weight control, calories always count. Take in more calories than your body uses and you will gain weight as the body stores fat; use more calories than you take in and the weight comes off. This is the principle behind all diets, whether they are low fat, low carb or any other combination of nutrients. To lose weight, you have to consume fewer calories than you burn!

Keep a note of what you eat and drink, and then look up each item in the calorie charts (or recipe pages) and add the figures together. To lose weight, you should try to keep within your daily calorie allowance; to gain weight you should aim to eat more than your daily calorie expenditure (see opposite). This book is about more than calories. It also gives you the amounts of fat, saturated fat, carbohydrate, protein and fibre per portion for each recipe and for all the food and drink items featured in the calorie tables. With this information you will see which nutrients each food contributes to your daily intake and so it will help you to plan a healthy diet. You will be able to tally your daily calorie and nutritional intake.

You can also use this book to help you plan your day's food, your weekly shopping and even your meals when eating out. Knowing the calorific value of foods in advance allows you to choose lower calorie and healthier options. Use it to compare similar types of foods or find out how many calories may be hidden in your favourite meals.

## Calorie counts

The foods and drinks in the calorie tables are grouped into categories – fruit, vegetables, bread and bakery, confectionery and ice cream, soft drinks, eating out and so on – to make it as easy as possible to locate a particular item. The foods in each category are listed alphabetically so that you can find them easily.

Calories and nutrients are given per standard portion to make life as easy as possible. It means that you don't have to weigh your food or calculate anything. But if you need to know the calories in a different-sized portion, multiply the calories given in this book by the weight of your portion, then divide by the weight given for the standard portion.

It has not been possible to include every food and every brand, but we have tried to give a representative sample of generic foods and brands under each category. If you cannot find a particular item here, you may be able to use the values for a similar product. The nutritional values are up to date at the time of publication but it should be noted that values may change from time to time, because manufacturers frequently change their formulations and amend recipes. Similarly, new products often appear on the supermarket shelves and existing ones are withdrawn.

### Start subtracting

As a rule of thumb, 3500 calories equals one pound of body fat. That means you have to take in 3500 fewer calories than you usually do over a period of time to lose one pound. Although its not 100% accurate (your metabolism and therefore weight loss typically slows over time), it can serve as a useful goal if you are trying to lose weight. By cutting 500 calories a day (a total of 3500 per week), and otherwise eating a balanced diet, you may find you lose approximately a pound a week. This rate of weight loss is considered reasonable and healthy.

### It's calories that count

Many diets restrict your intake of one particular nutrient, usually carbohydrates or fat. But the results of a 2012 study published in the American Journal of Clinical Nutrition suggest that when it comes to weight loss, it's simply calories that count (although, of course, eating a good balance of nutrients is important). Provided they stuck to their daily calorie allowance, dieters lost the same amount of weight in six months whether they cut carbs or fat, or upped protein. The key, it seems, is to find a plan that you can comfortably live with, rather than attempting to lose weight periodically with strict diets that are hard to maintain.

### What is a calorie?

Everyone talks about calories as if they are something contained in food. In fact, a calorie is a measure of energy, just as a kilo is a measure of weight and a mile is a measure of distance. In scientific terms, one calorie is the amount of energy (heat) required to increase the temperature of 1g of water by 1°C.

### Calories, kilocalories, kilojoules – what's the difference?

All of these terms crop up on food labels, which can be a bit confusing! Suffice to say that the scientifically defined calorie is a very small energy unit that is inconvenient to use because an average serving of any food typically provides thousands of these calories. For this reason, when speaking about food in the everyday sense, we say 'calorie' when we mean 'kilocalorie'; for example, a food label may declare a portion of food contains 100kcal but we would probably say 100 calories. You'll also see food energy measured in joules or kilojoules on food labels, which is the SI (International Unit System) unit for energy. 1 kcal is equivalent to 4.2kJ.

### How to reduce your calorie intake to kick-start weight loss

*1. Find your daily calorie expenditure*
Your calorie needs depend on your genetic make-up, age, weight, body composition, and your daily activity. They will differ from one day to the next and as you grow older. As a rough guide, it's around 2,000 calories a day for an average woman and 2,500 for a man. For a more accurate estimate of the number of calories you use during daily living and exercise, go to http://nutritiondata.self.com/tools/calories-burned and enter your gender, age, weight, height, lifestyle and details of daily exercise.

*2. Work out your daily calorie allowance*
Trim 500 calories off that total. For example, if your daily calorie burn is 2,000, then subtract 500 to get 1,500 calories. This is your daily calorie allowance, which will produce a weight loss of 0.5–1kg (1–2lb) per week. Don't try to lose more than this, otherwise you risk fatigue, excessive muscle loss and a significant drop in your metabolic rate, making weight loss harder. Record what you eat and tally your calorie intake with the help of this book.

## 12 Easy Calorie Swaps

By making a few easy swaps in your diet (see below) you can save calories and drop pounds. As a general rule, cut down on sugary, processed foods (such as cakes, biscuits, sweets and puddings) and sugary drinks. These foods are loaded with calories and are easy to over-consume without filling you up. Instead, choose unprocessed foods rich in nutrients and naturally filling: fruit, vegetables, salad, milk and dairy products, fish, lean meat, poultry and whole grains. Keep a check on portion sizes, especially when eating out, and always include the calories in drinks in your daily tally.

| Swap | For this | Save |
| --- | --- | --- |
| 1 slice (100g) cheesecake | 125g plain yogurt with 100g fruit | 300 |
| 1 slice apple pie | 110g stewed apples | 110 |
| 1 bag crisps (30g) | 30g plain popcorn | 100 |
| 1 rasher streaky bacon | 1 rasher trimmed back bacon | 40 |
| 1 slice (75g) chocolate cake | 1 apple | 295 |
| 1 Mars bar | 1 banana | 180 |
| Chicken korma (350g) | Chicken tikka (350g) | 230 |
| 2 digestive biscuits | 2 satsumas | 96 |
| 200ml apple juice | 200ml no added sugar squash | 76 |
| 330ml cola | water | 135 |

# A Healthy Diet

**Counting calories is important when you're trying to drop pounds, but you also need to make sure your diet is healthy and contains a good balance of nutrients. Here's what you need to eat each day.**

## Fat

Your body needs fat as it plays a critical role in heart health as well as providing fuel and helping to keep cell membranes healthy. It is also a source of vitamins A, D, E and K, and essential fatty acids (omega-3s and omega-6s), which the body cannot make itself.

All fats are high in calories (compared with carbohydrate and protein) so it is important to bear this in mind if you are watching your weight. However, this doesn't mean you have to cut it out from your diet completely. Gone are the days of extremely low fat diets. Studies have also shown that diets containing moderate amounts of fat (such as the Mediterranean diet) are more effective than a low fat diet in protecting against heart disease, stroke, type 2 diabetes, high blood cholesterol and high blood pressure. They have also proved a successful strategy for healthy weight loss. According to the National Health Service, adults should get 20 to 35 per cent of their total daily calories from fats.

But it's just as important to pay attention to the type of fat in your diet as it is to monitor your total fat. There are three main types of fat – saturated, monounsaturated and polyunsaturated – and most foods contain a combination of these three. Eat all fats in moderation, whether saturated or unsaturated, but avoid trans fats.

Monounsaturated fats are found in olive oil and rapeseed oil (and spreads made from these oils), as well as avocados, nuts, seeds and nut butters.

Polyunsaturated fats are found in sunflower, corn, safflower and soya oil and spreads made with oils as well as nuts and seeds, and oily fish.

Omega-3 and omega-6 fatty acids are both types of polyunsaturated oils. Omega-3 fatty acids are essential for regulating blood pressure and blood clotting and for boosting immunity. They help to reduce the risk of heart disease and are found in oily fish, walnuts, pumpkin seeds, flaxseed oil, rapeseed oil and omega-3 eggs. Omega-6 fatty acids are important for healthy skin and hormones. They are found in most vegetable oils, vegetable oil margarine, and products made from them. Use sparingly, as a high intake will block the uptake of omega-3 fats.

Saturated fats are mostly found in animal products (meat, sausages, burgers, bacon, egg yolk, butter, milk and cheese) as well as palm oil ('vegetable fat') and coconut oil. At the moment UK guidelines encourage us to swap some saturated for unsaturated fats. However, a recent study found no association between saturated fat and risk of heart disease. This suggests there's not enough evidence to back the current UK guidelines on the types of fat we eat.

### Trans fats

Avoid these wherever possible. Trans fats are found in hydrogenated fat, formed when hydrogen is added to liquid oils to make them solid. They increase blood levels of LDL cholesterol ('bad' cholesterol), harden your arteries and increase your risk of heart disease. Many manufacturers have removed these fats from many foods, but high levels may still be found in deep-fried fast foods, cakes, biscuits and doughnuts. Check the label for hydrogenated or partially hydrogenated fat.

## Protein

We need to eat protein to make and repair body cells, as well as to manufacture enzymes, hormones and antibodies. The richest sources include meat, fish, poultry, eggs, milk, cheese and yogurt, and good levels are also found in beans, lentils, nuts, seeds, Quorn, tofu and cereals.

## Carbohydrate

Carbohydrate (sugars and starch) provides energy for daily activities and exercise. Your brain, nervous system and heart need a constant supply of carbohydrate to function properly. Generally, carbohydrate in fibre-rich unprocessed foods, such as wholegrains, potatoes, beans, lentils, fruit and vegetables, provide longer-lasting energy and help you feel full for longer. These foods should make up most of your carbohydrate intake.

## Fibre

The digestive system requires fibre from foods for it to work properly, and fibre is also useful for weight control. There are two kinds: insoluble and soluble. Most plant foods contain both, but proportions vary. Good sources of insoluble fibre include whole grains (such as brown rice, wholemeal bread) and vegetables. These foods help speed the passage of food through your gut, preventing constipation and bowel problems, and they make you feel full after eating. Soluble fibre – found in oats, beans, lentils, fruit and vegetables – reduces harmful LDL cholesterol levels, and it helps to control blood glucose levels by slowing glucose absorption. It also reduces hunger and improves appetite control. A healthy diet should contain at least 18g (¾oz) a day.

## Salt and sodium

On a food label, salt is often listed as sodium, and 1g of sodium is roughly the same as 2.5g of salt. It's the sodium that can lead to health problems such as high blood pressure, increasing your risk of stroke and coronary heart disease. Adults should not have more than 6g (about 1 tsp) of salt per day.

## The eatwell plate

To help you eat healthily, the government has devised an eating system called the eatwell plate, based on the five food groups:
- Bread, rice, potatoes, pasta and other starchy foods
- Fruit and vegetables
- Milk and dairy foods
- Meat, fish, eggs, beans and other non-dairy sources of protein
- Foods and drinks high in fat and/or sugar

The eatwell plate shows the different types of food you need to eat – and in what proportions – to have a well-balanced and healthy diet. You should try to eat a wide variety of foods from the first four groups every day, and limit the amount you eat from the fifth group.

### Bread, rice, potatoes, pasta and other starchy foods
*Eat these foods at each meal*
These foods should make up roughly a third of the food you eat. Try to choose wholegrain varieties where you can, such as wholemeal bread and pasta, wholegrain breakfast cereals and wholegrain rice. A portion is:
- 2 slices of bread
- 5 tablespoons (180g) pasta or rice
- 40g bowl of breakfast cereal
- 1 fist-sized (150g) potato

### Fruit and vegetables
*Eat at least 5 portions a day*
These foods should make up about a third of the food you eat each day. Aim to eat a variety of fruit and vegetables each day. Fresh, frozen, tinned, dried and juiced all count. A portion is 80g or any of these:
- 1 apple, banana, pear or orange
- 2 small fruits e.g. satsumas, plums, apricots
- 3 heaped tablespoons of vegetables
- a dessert bowl of salad
- a glass (150ml) of fruit juice (counts as a maximum of one portion a day)

### Milk and dairy foods
*Eat 2 or 3 portions a day*
Foods in this group include milk, cheese and yogurt. Choose lower-fat options where available, such as skimmed milk. Or you could have just a small amount of the high-fat varieties less often.
A portion is:
- 200ml milk
- A small pot of yogurt
- A matchbox sized (40g) piece of cheese

### Meat, fish, eggs, beans and other non-dairy sources of protein
*Eat 2 portions a day*
Try to eat some foods from this group each day and aim for at least two portions of fish a week, including a portion of oily fish. Some types of meat can be high in saturated fat so try to choose leaner cuts where possible and trim excess fat. Beans, peas and lentils are good alternatives to meat because they're naturally low in fat, and they're high in fibre, protein, and vitamins and minerals.
A portion is:
- A piece of meat, chicken or fish the size of a deck of cards (70g)
- 2 eggs
- 2 heaped tablespoons of beans or lentils
- 2 tablespoons (25g) nuts or seeds

### Foods and drinks high in fat and/or sugar
*Eat only small amounts of these foods*
These foods include cakes, biscuits, spreads, crisps, sugar, confectionery and soft drinks. Cutting down on these types of food could help you control your weight because they contain lots of calories.

## Vitamins and minerals

Vitamins support the immune system, help the brain function and convert food into energy. They are important for healthy skin and hair, controlling growth and balancing hormones. Some vitamins – the B vitamins and vitamin C – must be provided by the diet daily, as they cannot be stored. Minerals are needed for structural and regulatory functions, including bone strength, haemoglobin manufacture, fluid balance and muscle contraction.

| Mineral | Use | Best food sources |
| --- | --- | --- |
| Calcium | Builds bone and teeth. For blood clotting, nerve and muscle function | Milk and dairy products; sardines; dark green leafy vegetables; pulses; Brazil nuts; almonds; figs; sesame seeds |
| Iron | For the formation of red blood cells and for oxygen transport. Prevents anaemia | Meat and offal; wholegrain cereals; fortified breakfast cereals; pulses; green leafy vegetables; nuts; sesame and pumpkin seeds |
| Zinc | For a healthy immune system, wound healing, and skin and cell growth | Eggs; wholegrain cereals; meat; nuts and seeds |
| Magnesium | For healthy bones, muscle and nerve function and for cell formation | Cereals; fruit; vegetables; milk; nuts and seeds |
| Potassium | For fluid balance, and for muscle and nerve function | Fruit; vegetables; cereals; nuts and seeds |
| Sodium | For fluid balance, and for muscle and nerve function | Salt; processed meat; ready meals; sauces; soup; cheese; bread |
| Selenium | An antioxidant that helps protect against heart disease and cancer | Cereals; vegetables; dairy products |

| Vitamin | Use | Best food sources |
| --- | --- | --- |
| A | For vision in dim light; healthy skin and linings of the digestive tract, nose and throat | Full-fat dairy products; meat; offal; oily fish; margarine |
| Beta-carotene | An antioxidant that protects against certain cancers; converts into vitamin A | Fruit and vegetables e.g. apricots, peppers, tomatoes, mangoes, broccoli, squash, carrots, watercress |
| Vitamin B1 (thiamin) | Releases energy from carbohydrates. For healthy nerves and digestive system | Wholemeal bread and cereals; pulses; meat; sunflower seeds |
| Vitamin B2 (riboflavin) | Releases energy from carbohydrates. For healthy skin, eyes and nerves. | Milk and dairy products; meat; eggs, soya products |
| Vitamin B3 (niacin) | Releases energy from carbohydrates. For healthy skin, nerves and digestion | Meat and offal; nuts; milk and dairy products; eggs; wholegrain cereals |
| Vitamin B6 (pyridoxine) | Metabolises protein, carbohydrate, fat. For red blood cell manufacture and a healthy immune system | Pulses; nuts; eggs; cereals; fish; bananas |
| Folic acid | Formation of DNA and red blood cells. Reduces risk of spina bifida in developing babies | Green leafy vegetables; yeast extract; pulses; nuts; citrus fruit |
| Vitamin B12 | Formation of red blood cells. For energy metabolism | Milk and dairy products; meat; fish; fortified breakfast cereals; soya products; yeast extract |
| Vitamin C | Healthy connective tissue, bones, teeth, blood vessels, gums and teeth. Promotes immune function. Helps iron absorption | Fruit and vegetables e.g. raspberries, blackcurrants, kiwi, oranges, peppers, broccoli, cabbage, tomatoes |
| Vitamin D | Builds strong bones. Needed to absorb calcium and phosphorus | Sunlight; oily fish; fortified margarine and breakfast cereals; eggs |
| Vitamin E | Antioxidant which helps protect against heart disease; promotes normal cell growth and development | Vegetable oils; oily fish; nuts; seeds; egg yolk; avocado |

# How To Read Food Labels

**Food labels provide useful information, but they can be confusing. Here's how to decipher them.**

### Read the list of ingredients

These are listed in descending order of weight; that is, the most to the least. If an ingredient is mentioned in the name of the product, such as the apple in 'apple pie', or is shown on the label, the amount of the ingredient in the food must be given as a percentage.

### Read the nutrition label

The nutrients below must be listed per 100g or per 100ml:

- Energy (Kcals)
- Protein (g)
- Fat (g)
- Carbohydrate (g)

Food manufacturers can include more nutritional information, but if a food product makes a health claim for a specific nutrient, the relevant information must be listed; for example, if a food is described as low salt, the salt content must be given.

### Traffic light labelling

Traffic light labels are the Food Standards Agency-approved labelling system, and they tell you whether the food has high, medium or low amounts of each of the listed nutrients in 100g of the food: Green is used to show the food is low in that nutrient; Amber signals that the product contains medium levels of that nutrient; and Red represents high amounts and warns shoppers not to consume much. Many of the foods with traffic light colours will have a mixture of red, amber and greens. The idea is, when you're choosing between similar products, to go for more greens and ambers, and fewer reds.

|  | **Men** | **Women** |
|---|---|---|
| **Fat (total)** | 95g | 70g |
| **Of which saturates** | 30g | 20g |
| **Salt** | 6g | 6g |
| **Sugar*** | 120g | 90g |

* Total sugars includes sugars occurring naturally in foods as well as added sugars

### Guideline Daily Amounts (GDAs)

GDAs are a guide to how much energy and key nutrients the average healthy person needs in order to have a balanced diet. The GDAs for the most important nutrients listed on food labels are as above.

GDAs show how much of that nutrient is in a portion of food and are a guide and a maximum. If you are a normal weight you can aim to reach the GDA for calories, but try to eat no more than the GDAs for fat, saturates, salt and sugars.

## Read the nutrition claims

It's important to understand the claims below, because a chocolate rice breakfast cereal, for example, could claim to be low in fat, but it could also be high in sugar and calories. A general rule is to treat these claims with caution. Something that claims to be lower in fat may still contain the same number of calories as other versions. It is best to decide whether a food is suitable by comparing the nutritional information of products.

| | |
|---|---|
| **'Low calorie'** | Contains less than 40 calories per 100g |
| **'Reduced calorie'** | Contains at least 25% less than the standard version |
| **'Low fat'** | Contains less than 3g of fat per 100g (for food) or 1.5g of fat per 100ml (for liquids) |
| **'Reduced fat'** | Contains 25% less fat than a similar product |
| **'Less than 5% fat'** | Contains less than 5g of fat per 100g of the food |
| **'No added sugar'** | No sugars have been added as an ingredient. But the product may still contain high levels of natural sugars from e.g. fruit juice or dried fruit |
| **'Low sugar'** | Contains no more than 5g sugar per 100g |
| **'Reduced sugar'** | Contains 25% less sugar than a similar product |
| **'Lite' or 'light'** | No legal definition |

# UNDER 300
# CALORIES

# Tropical Fruit Pots

Preparation time 15 minutes • Cooking time 5 minutes • Serves 8 • Per Serving 192 calories, 1g fat (of which trace saturates), 45g carbohydrates, 4g protein, 3g fibre, 0.1g salt

**400g can apricots in fruit juice**
**2 balls of preserved stem ginger**
  **in syrup, finely chopped, plus**
  **2 tbsp syrup from the jar**
**½ tsp ground cinnamon**
**juice of 1 orange**
**3 oranges, cut into segments**
**1 mango, peeled, stoned and**
  **chopped**
**1 pineapple, peeled, core removed,**
  **and chopped**
**450g (1lb) coconut yogurt**
**3 tbsp lemon curd**
**3–4 tbsp light muscovado sugar**

**1.** Drain the juice from the apricots into a pan and stir in the syrup from the ginger, then add the chopped ginger, the cinnamon and orange juice. Put over a low heat and stir gently. Bring to the boil, then reduce the heat and simmer for 2–3 minutes to make a thick syrup.

**2.** Roughly chop the apricots and put into a bowl with the segmented oranges, the mango and pineapple. Pour the syrup over the fruit. Divide among eight 300ml (½ pint) glasses or bowls.

**3.** Beat the yogurt and lemon curd together in a bowl until smooth. Spoon a generous dollop over the fruit and sprinkle with muscovado sugar. Chill if not serving immediately.

**GET AHEAD**
*Complete the recipe to the end of step 2 up to 2 hours before you plan to eat – no need to chill.*

# Berry Breakfast

Preparation time 15 minute, plus overnight chilling • Cooking time 10 minutes, plus cooling • Serves 4
Per Serving 156 calories, trace fat, 40g carbohydrates, 1g protein, 2g fibre, 0g salt

**175g (6oz) raspberry conserve**
**juice of 1 orange**
**juice of 1 lemon**
**1 tsp rosewater**
**350g (12oz) strawberries, hulled
and thickly sliced**
**150g (5oz) blueberries**

**1.** Put the raspberry conserve into a pan with the orange and lemon juices and add 150ml (¼ pint) boiling water. Stir over a low heat to dissolve the conserve, then leave to cool.

**2.** Stir in the rosewater and taste – you may want to add a squeeze more lemon juice if it's too sweet. Put the strawberries and blueberries into a serving bowl and strain the raspberry conserve mixture over them. Cover and chill overnight. Take out of the fridge about 30 minutes before serving.

# Porridge with Dried Fruit

Preparation time 5 minutes • Cooking time 5 minutes • Serves 4 • Per Serving 279 calories, 6g fat (of which 1g saturates), 49g carbohydrates, 10g protein, 5g fibre, 0.2g salt

**200g (7oz) porridge oats**
**400ml (14fl oz) milk, plus extra**
  **to serve**
**75g (3oz) mixture of chopped dried**
  **figs, apricots and raisins**

1. Put the oats into a large pan and add the milk and 400ml (14fl oz) water. Stir in the figs, apricots and raisins and heat gently, stirring until the porridge thickens and the oats are cooked.

2. Divide among four bowls and serve with a splash of milk.

# Breakfast Bruschetta

Preparation time 5 minutes • Cooking time 5 minutes • Serves 4 • Per Serving 145 calories,
1g fat (of which 0g saturates), 30g carbohydrates, 11g protein, 5g fibre, 0.4g salt

**1 ripe banana, peeled and sliced**
**250g (9oz) blueberries**
**200g (7oz) quark cheese**
**4 slices pumpernickel or wheat-**
    **free wholegrain bread**
**1 tbsp runny honey**

**1.** Put the banana into a bowl with the blueberries. Spoon in the quark cheese and mix well.

**2.** Toast the slices of bread on both sides, then spread with the blueberry mixture. Drizzle with the honey and serve immediately.

**HEALTHY TIP**

*This breakfast idea is very low in fat. Pumpernickel bread is made from rye flour, which is rich in fibre, iron and zinc. It has a lower GI than bread made from wheat flour, which means it provides a sustained energy boost to see you through the morning. The blueberries are rich in anthocyanins, which help combat heart disease, certain cancers and stroke.*

# French Toast

Preparation time 5 minutes • Cooking time 10 minutes • Serves 4 • Per Serving 259 calories, 20g fat (of which 9g saturates), 15g carbohydrates, 8g protein, 0.5g fibre, 0.7g salt

**2 medium eggs**
**150ml (¼ pint) semi-skimmed milk**
**a generous pinch of freshly grated nutmeg or ground cinnamon**
**4 slices white bread, or fruit bread, crusts removed and each slice cut into four fingers**
**50g (2oz) butter**
**vegetable oil for frying**
**1 tbsp golden caster sugar**

**1.** Put the eggs, milk and nutmeg or cinnamon into a shallow dish and beat together.

**2.** Dip the pieces of bread into the mixture, coating them well.

**3.** Heat half the butter with 1 tbsp oil in a heavy-based frying pan. When the butter is foaming, fry the egg-coated bread pieces in batches, until golden on both sides, adding more butter and oil as needed. Sprinkle with sugar and serve.

**COOK'S TIP**

*Use leftover bread for this tasty breakfast or brunch dish. For a savoury version, use white bread and omit the spice and sugar; serve with tomato ketchup, or with bacon and maple syrup.*

# Poached Eggs with Mushrooms

Preparation time 15 minutes • Cooking time 20 minutes • Serves 4 • Per Serving 263 calories, 21g fat (of which 8g saturates), 1g carbohydrates, 19g protein, 2g fibre, 0.7g salt

**8 medium-sized flat or portabella mushrooms**
**25g (1oz) butter**
**8 medium eggs**
**225g (8oz) baby spinach leaves**
**4 level tsp (20g) fresh pesto**

1. Preheat the oven to 200°C (180°C fan oven) mark 6. Arrange the mushrooms in a single layer in a small roasting tin and dot with the butter. Roast for 15 minutes or until golden brown and soft.

2. Meanwhile, bring a wide shallow pan of water to the boil. When the mushrooms are half-cooked and the water is bubbling furiously, break the eggs into the pan, spaced well apart, then take the pan off the heat. The eggs will take about 6 minutes to cook.

3. When the mushrooms are tender, put them on a warmed plate, cover and put back into the turned-off oven to keep warm.

4. Put the roasting tin over a medium heat on the hob and add the spinach. Cook, stirring, for about 30 seconds or until the spinach has just started to wilt.

5. The eggs should be set by now, so divide the mushrooms among four warmed plates and top with a little spinach, a poached egg and a teaspoonful of pesto.

**HEALTHY TIP**
*Eggs once had a bad press with many people believing (wrongly) that they raised blood cholesterol levels. However, scientists have found that most people can safely eat up to two eggs a day without any adverse effect on their cholesterol levels.*

# Huevos Rancheros

Preparation time 10 minutes • Cooking time 15 minutes • Serves 6 • Per Serving 122 calories,
7g fat (of which 1g saturates), 9g carbohydrates, 7g protein, 2g fibre, 0.3g salt

1 tbsp vegetable oil,
1 medium red onion, finely sliced
1 each yellow and red pepper,
   seeded and finely sliced
1 red chilli, seeded and finely
   sliced
2 × 400g cans chopped tomatoes
½ tsp dried mixed herbs
4 large eggs
salt and freshly ground black
   pepper
a small handful of fresh flat-leafed
   parsley, roughly chopped,
   to garnish

1. Heat the oil in a large frying pan over a high heat. Add the onion, peppers and chilli and fry for 3 minutes until just softened. Add the tomatoes and dried herbs. Season with salt and ground black pepper and simmer for 3 minutes.

2. Break an egg into a small cup. Use a wooden spoon to scrape a hole in the tomato mixture, then quickly drop in the egg. Repeat with the remaining eggs, spacing evenly around the tomato mixture. Cover and simmer for 3–5 minutes until the eggs are just set. Sprinkle with parsley and serve.

**GOES WELL WITH...**
*crusty bread*

# Chicken & Dumpling Soup

Preparation time 20 minutes • Cooking time 25 minutes • Serves 6 • Per Serving 278 calories, 12g fat (of which 3g saturates), 18g carbohydrates, 25g protein, 3g fibre, 1.2g salt

**1½ tbsp olive oil**
**1 medium onion, finely chopped**
**2 carrots, finely diced**
**3 celery sticks, finely diced**
**1 garlic clove, crushed**
**1.6 litres (2¾ pints) chicken stock**
**500g (1lb 2oz) skinless chicken thigh fillets, cut into finger-size strips**
**1 leek, trimmed and sliced into rings**
**100g (3½oz) plain flour**
**½ tsp baking powder**
**a large handful of fresh parsley, chopped**
**5 tbsp semi-skimmed milk**
**salt and freshly ground black pepper**

1. Heat ½ tbsp of the oil in a pan. Add the onion, carrots and celery and fry for 10 minutes until softened. Stir in the garlic and cook for 1 minute.

2. Pour in the stock and bring to the boil. Add the chicken and leek, bring back to the boil, reduce the heat and simmer for 6 minutes or until the chicken is cooked and the vegetables are just tender.

3. Meanwhile, put the flour into a medium bowl. Stir in the baking powder, some parsley and plenty of seasoning. Add the remaining oil and milk and stir together until just combined to make a rough, slightly sticky dough.

4. Drop small teaspoonfuls of the dumpling mixture into the simmering stock and cook for 4 minutes (the dumplings will swell up, so don't make them too big). Check the seasoning.

5. Ladle the soup and dumplings into warmed soup bowls, then garnish with the remaining parsley and serve.

# Vietnamese Turkey Noodle Soup

Preparation time 15 minutes • Cooking time 10 minutes • Serves 4 • Per Serving 284 calories, 3g fat (of which 1g saturates), 22g carbohydrates, 43g protein, 3g fibre, 1.7g salt

1.8–2 litres (3¼–3½ pints) chicken stock
4cm (1½in) fresh root ginger, peeled and finely chopped
1 garlic clove, finely chopped
450g (1lb) turkey breast fillet, sliced into thin strips
1 tbsp fish sauce
¼ head Savoy cabbage, finely shredded
100g (3½oz) rice noodles
a large handful of bean sprouts
juice of 1 lime
1 large red chilli, seeded and thinly sliced
4 spring onions, sliced
salt and freshly ground black pepper
a large handful each of fresh coriander and mint, roughly chopped, to garnish

1. Bring the stock to the boil in a large pan. Add the ginger, garlic and turkey and simmer for 5 minutes.

2. Stir in the fish sauce, cabbage and noodles and cook for 3 minutes (check the turkey is cooked). Add the bean sprouts, lime juice and most of the chilli and spring onions. Check the seasoning. Divide among four bowls, garnish with the herbs, remaining chilli and spring onions. Serve immediately.

# Healthy Fish Chowder

Preparation time 20 minutes • Cooking time 25 minutes • Serves 4 • Per Serving 274 calories, 9g fat (of which 3g saturates), 31g carbohydrates, 20g protein, 2g fibre, 2g salt

1 tbsp olive oil

1 onion, finely chopped

1 celery stick, finely chopped

500ml (18fl oz) hot vegetable or fish stock

250ml (9fl oz) skimmed milk

200g (7oz) baby new potatoes, halved

150g (5oz) skinless smoked haddock, diced

150g (5oz) skinless white fish, such as cod or pollack, diced

2 × 198g cans sweetcorn, drained

2 tbsp double cream

2 tbsp freshly chopped chives

salt and freshly ground black pepper

1. Heat the oil in a large pan over a medium heat. Add the onion and celery and gently fry for about 10 minutes until soft and translucent.

2. Add the hot stock and milk, then bring to the boil. Add the potatoes, then reduce the heat and simmer for 10 minutes or until the vegetables are tender.

3. Stir in the fish, sweetcorn and some seasoning and simmer for 3–5 minutes until the fish is cooked. Carefully stir through the cream and most of the chives and check the seasoning. Garnish with the remaining chives and serve.

# Warming Veggie Minestrone

Preparation time 15 minutes • Cooking time 25 minutes • Serves 4 • Per Serving 278 calories, 5g fat (of which 1g saturates), 46g carbohydrates, 13g protein, 13g fibre, 1.7g salt

**1 onion, roughly chopped**
**2 celery sticks, roughly chopped**
**4 small carrots, roughly chopped**
**1 tbsp vegetable oil**
**400g can chopped tomatoes**
**1.4 litres (2½ pints) vegetable stock**
**125g (4oz) spaghetti, broken into small pieces**
**410g can cannellini beans, drained and rinsed**
**150g (5oz) frozen peas**
**salt and freshly ground black pepper**
**a small handful of fresh basil to garnish**

**1.** Pulse the onion, celery and carrots in a food processor until chopped to the size of peas. Heat the oil in a large pan and fry the chopped vegetables over a medium heat for 10 minutes until soft. Add the tomatoes and stock and bring to a simmer.

**2.** Mix in the spaghetti and simmer for 10 minutes, adding the beans and peas for the final 3 minutes. Check the seasoning and ladle into bowls. Garnish with basil and serve.

**GOES WELL WITH...**
*crusty bread*

# Butternut Squash Soup with Cheesy Toasts

Preparation time 30 minutes • Cooking time 35 minutes • Serves 6 • Per Serving 250 calories, 11g fat (of which 4g saturates), 32g carbohydrates, 19g protein, 5g fibre, 1.3g salt

**FOR THE SOUP**

**2 tbsp extra virgin olive oil, plus extra to drizzle**

**5 fresh sage leaves**

**1 large onion, finely chopped**

**2 celery sticks, finely chopped**

**2 medium carrots, finely chopped**

**1 butternut squash, about 900g (2lb), peeled, seeded and cut into rough 2.5cm (1in pieces)**

**1.3 litres (2¼ pints) vegetable stock**

**salt and freshly ground black pepper**

**FOR THE CHEESY TOASTS**

**6 slices bread**

**100g (3½oz) Cheddar or Parmesan, grated**

**few pinches dried chilli flakes**

**few dashes Worcestershire sauce (optional)**

**1.** Heat the oil in a large pan and add the sage leaves. Cook for 30 seconds or until crisp. Lift out the leaves with a slotted spoon (leaving any oil behind) and put on kitchen paper (the leaves will be used as a garnish).

**2.** To the pan, add the onion, celery, carrots and squash. Cook for 10 minutes, stirring occasionally, until the vegetables are beginning to soften. Pour in the stock and bring to the boil, then reduce the heat and simmer gently for 20 minutes or until the vegetables are completely soft.

**3.** Whiz the soup in a blender (in batches if necessary) until smooth, then pour back into the pan. Check the seasoning and put to one side.

**4.** To make the cheesy toasts, preheat the grill to medium. Lay the bread slices out on a baking tray, then grill on both sides until toasted and lightly golden. Divide the cheese, chilli flakes and Worcestershire sauce, if using, among the toasts and grill until golden and bubbling. Reheat the soup if necessary and ladle into six warmed soup bowls. Garnish with a drizzle of oil and the crumbled fried sage leaves. Serve with the cheesy toasts.

**FREEZING TIP**

*To make ahead and freeze, prepare the soup to the end of step 3 (no need to fry the sage). Leave the soup to cool completely; transfer to a freezeproof container or bag, cover if needed and freeze for up to six months. To serve, thaw the soup; reheat gently in a pan (frying the sage in a little oil) and complete the recipe to serve.*

# Throw-it-all-together Salad

Preparation time 10 minutes • Serves 4 • Per Serving 255 calories, 13g fat (of which 3g saturates), 7g carbohydrates, 29g protein, 2g fibre, 0.8g salt

**2–4 chargrilled chicken breasts, torn into strips**
**2 carrots, peeled into strips**
**½ cucumber, halved lengthways, seeded and cut into ribbons**
**a handful of fresh coriander leaves, roughly chopped**
**½ head of Chinese leaves, shredded**
**4 handfuls of watercress**
**4 spring onions, shredded**

**FOR THE DRESSING**
**5 tbsp peanut butter**
**2 tbsp sweet chilli sauce**
**juice of 1 lime**
**salt and freshly ground black pepper**

1. Put all the salad ingredients into a large salad bowl.

2. To make the dressing, put the peanut butter, chilli sauce and lime juice in a small bowl and mix together well. Season with salt and pepper. Add 2–3 tbsp cold water, a tablespoon at a time, to thin the dressing if it's too thick to pour. Use just enough water to make the dressing the right consistency.

3. Drizzle the dressing over the salad, toss together and serve.

# Deluxe Fig & Ham Salad

Preparation time 10 minutes • Cooking time about 10 minutes • Serves 4 • Per Serving 252 calories, 12g fat (of which 2g saturates), 26g carbohydrates, 11g protein, 3g fibre, 1.7g salt

**200g (7oz) fine green beans, ends trimmed**

**3 tbsp extra virgin olive oil**

**4 slices white sourdough bread, cut into large cubes**

**4 little gem lettuces, quartered lengthways**

**85g pack of Parma ham**

**4 figs, quartered**

**1 tsp Dijon mustard**

**½ tbsp cider or white wine vinegar**

**salt and freshly ground black pepper**

1. Bring a small pan of water to the boil and cook the beans for 4 minutes or until tender. Drain and leave in a colander to steam dry until needed.

2. Heat 1 tbsp of the oil in a large frying pan and fry the bread cubes, tossing frequently, until golden and crisp. Season with salt and leave to cool.

3. Arrange the lettuce quarters, cut side up, on a large platter. Roughly rip the Parma ham slices in half lengthways and weave among the lettuce quarters. Dot the figs, beans and toasted bread cubes over the top.

4. In a small jug, mix together the mustard, vinegar, remaining oil and some seasoning. Drizzle over the salad and serve.

# Chilli Beef Noodle Salad

Preparation time 15 minutes, plus soaking • Serves 4 • Per Serving 286 calories, 11g fat (of which 2g saturates), 33g carbohydrates, 12g protein, 0.6g fibre, 0.8g salt

**150g (5oz) dried rice noodles**
**50g (2oz) rocket**
**125g (4oz) sliced cold roast beef**
**125g (4oz) sunblush or sundried tomatoes, chopped**

**FOR THE THAI DRESSING**
**juice of 1 lime**
**1 lemongrass stalk, outside leaves discarded, trimmed and finely chopped**
**1 red chilli, seeded and chopped**
**2 tsp finely chopped fresh root ginger**
**2 garlic cloves, crushed**
**1 tbsp Thai fish sauce**
**3 tbsp extra virgin olive oil**
**salt and freshly ground black pepper**

1. Put the noodles into a large bowl and pour boiling water over them to cover. Put to one side for 15 minutes.

2. To make the dressing, whisk together the lime juice, lemongrass, chilli, ginger, garlic, fish sauce and oil in a small bowl and season with salt and ground black pepper.

3. While they are still warm, drain the noodles well, put into a large bowl and toss with the dressing. Leave to cool.

4. Toss the rocket, sliced beef and tomatoes through the noodles and serve.

# Hot Smoked Salmon Salad

Preparation time 15 minutes • Cooking time 8 minutes • Serves 4 • Per Serving 282 calories, 11g fat (of which 2g saturates), 27g carbohydrates, 27g protein, 3g fibre, 3.3g salt

**4 medium eggs**
**300g (11oz) small new potatoes, quartered**
**200g (7oz) fine green beans, trimmed and halved**
**100g (3½oz) radishes, thinly sliced**
**80g bag salad leaves**
**50g (2oz) ready-made croûtons**
**250g (9oz) hot-smoked salmon, skinned and flaked**

**FOR THE DRESSING**
**3 tbsp sweet chilli sauce**
**1 tbsp freshly chopped chives**
**2 tbsp extra virgin olive oil**
**salt and freshly ground black pepper**

**1.** Bring two small pans of water to the boil. To one, add the eggs, reduce the heat and simmer for 7 minutes. To the other, add the potatoes and beans and cook for 6 minutes until tender.

**2.** Meanwhile, put the radishes into a large bowl with the salad leaves, croûtons and salmon flakes. In a small bowl, mix together the dressing ingredients with some seasoning.

**3.** Drain the potatoes and beans and leave to steam-dry in a colander. Lift out the eggs and run under cold water then shell and quarter. Add the potatoes and beans to the salad bowl and toss gently. Divide the salad mixture among four plates and top each with a quartered egg. Drizzle over the dressing and serve with

**GET AHEAD**
*Boil and drain the eggs, potatoes and beans, then chill until needed.*

# Broad Bean & Feta Salad

Preparation time 10 minutes • Cooking time about 5 minutes • Serves 2 • Per Serving 197 calories,
16g fat (of which 4g saturates), 5g carbohydrates, 14g protein, 6g fibre, 1.3g salt

**225g (8oz) podded broad beans
    (see Cook's Tip )**
**100g (3½oz) feta cheese, chopped**
**2 tbsp freshly chopped mint**
**2 tbsp extra virgin olive oil**
**a squeeze of lemon juice**
**salt and freshly ground black
    pepper**

**1.** Cook the beans in salted boiling water for 3–5 minutes until tender. Drain, then plunge them into cold water and drain again. Remove their skins if you like (see Cook's Tip).

**2.** Tip the beans into a bowl and add the feta, mint, oil and a squeeze of lemon juice. Season well with salt and ground black pepper, toss together and serve.

**GOES WELL WITH...**
*extra lemon wedges to squeeze over the salad*

**COOK'S TIP**
*For this quantity of broad beans, you will need to buy about 750g (1½lb) beans in pods. Choose small pods, as the beans will be young and will have a better flavour than bigger, older beans. Very young broad beans, less than 7.5cm (3in) long, can be cooked in their pods and eaten whole. Pod older beans and skin them to remove the outer coat, which toughens with age. To do this, slip the beans out of their skins after blanching.*

# Sprouted Bean & Mango Salad

Preparation time 15 minutes • Serves 6 • Per Serving 115 calories, 4g fat (of which 0.7g saturates), 17g carbohydrates, 2g protein, 3g fibre, 0.5g salt

**3 tbsp mango chutney**

**grated zest and juice of 1 lime**

**2 tbsp olive oil**

**4 plum tomatoes**

**1 small red onion, chopped**

**1 red pepper, seeded and finely diced**

**1 yellow pepper, seeded and finely diced**

**1 mango, peeled, stoned and finely diced**

**4 tbsp freshly chopped coriander**

**150g (5oz) sprouted beans (see Cook's Tip)**

**salt and freshly ground black pepper**

**1.** To make the dressing, place the mango chutney in a small bowl and add the lime zest and juice. Whisk in the oil and season with salt and ground black pepper.

**2.** Quarter the tomatoes, discard the seeds and then cut into dice. Put into a large bowl with the onion, peppers, mango, coriander and sprouted beans. Pour the dressing over and mix well. Serve the salad immediately.

**COOK'S TIP**

*Many beans and seeds can be sprouted at home, but buy ones that are specifically produced for sprouting. Mung beans take five to six days to sprout. Allow 125g (4oz) bean sprouts per person.*

# Panzanella Salad

Preparation time 20 minutes, plus standing • Serves 4 • Per Serving 228 calories, 14g fat (of which 3g saturates), 21g carbohydrates, 6g protein, 2g fibre, 0.6g salt

**2–3 thick slices from a day-old country loaf (total weight about 100g/3½oz), torn or cut into cubes**
**450g (1lb) ripe tomatoes, roughly chopped**
**2 tbsp capers**
**1 tsp freshly chopped thyme**
**1 small red onion, thinly sliced**
**2 garlic cloves**
**2 small red chillies, seeded and finely chopped**
**4 tbsp extra virgin olive oil**
**125g (4oz) pitted black olives**
**50g (2oz) sun-dried tomatoes, roughly chopped**
**8 fresh basil leaves**
**25g (1oz) Parmesan, pared into shavings with a vegetable peeler**
**salt and freshly ground black pepper**
**fresh thyme sprigs to garnish**

**1.** Put the bread into a large bowl with the tomatoes, capers, chopped thyme, onion, garlic, chillies, oil, olives and sun-dried tomatoes. Season well with salt and ground black pepper, then toss together and leave in a cool place for 30 minutes.

**2.** Toss the salad thoroughly again. Tear the basil into pieces and scatter over the salad with the Parmesan shavings. Garnish with thyme sprigs, then serve.

**COOK'S TIP**
*This salad is best made two or three hours ahead to let the flavours mingle.*

# Sardines on Toast

Preparation time 5 minutes • Cooking time about 10 minutes • Serves 4 • Per Serving 173 calories, 7g fat (of which 2g saturates), 13g carbohydrates, 14g protein, 3g fibre, 0.9g salt

**4 thick slices wholemeal bread**
**2 large tomatoes, sliced**
**2 × 120g cans sardines in olive oil, drained**
**juice of ½ lemon**
**freshly ground black pepper**
**a small handful of fresh parsley, chopped, to garnish**

**1.** Preheat the grill. Toast the bread on both sides.

**2.** Divide the tomato slices and the sardines among the toast slices, squeeze the lemon juice over them, then put back under the grill for 2–3 minutes to heat through. Season with ground black pepper, then scatter the parsley over the sardines to garnish and serve immediately.

# Mozzarella Mushrooms

Preparation time 5 minutes • Cooking time about 20 minutes • Serves 4 • Per Serving 234 calories, 9g fat (of which 5g saturates), 25g carbohydrates, 14g protein, 3g fibre, 0.4g salt

**8 large portabella mushrooms**
**8 slices marinated red pepper**
**8 fresh basil leaves**
**150g (5oz) mozzarella cheese, cut into 8 slices**
**4 English muffins, halved**
**salt and freshly ground black pepper**

**1.** Preheat the oven to 200°C (180°C fan oven) mark 6. Lay the mushrooms side by side in a roasting tin and season with salt and ground black pepper. Top each mushroom with a slice of red pepper and a basil leaf. Lay a slice of mozzarella on top of each mushroom and season again. Roast for 15–20 minutes until the mushrooms are tender and the cheese has melted.

**2.** Meanwhile, toast the muffin halves until golden. Put a mozzarella mushroom on top of each muffin half. Serve immediately.

**GOES WELL WITH...**
*green salad*

**HEALTHY TIP**
*Mushrooms are an excellent source of potassium – a mineral that helps lower elevated blood pressure and reduces the risk of stroke. One medium portabella mushroom has even more potassium than a banana or a glass of orange juice. Mushrooms contain antioxidant nutrients that help inhibit the development of cancers of the breast and prostate.*

# Spicy Beans & Potatoes

Preparation time 12 minutes • Cooking time about 1½ hours • Serves 4 • Per Serving 276 calories, 4g fat (of which 1g saturates), 56g carbohydrates, 10g protein, 7g fibre, 0.8g salt

**4 baking potatoes**
**1 tbsp olive oil, plus extra to rub**
**1 tsp smoked paprika, plus a pinch**
**2 shallots, finely chopped**
**1 tbsp freshly chopped rosemary**
**400g can cannellini beans, drained**
**and rinsed**
**400g can chopped tomatoes**
**1 tbsp light muscovado sugar**
**1 tsp Worcestershire sauce**
**75ml (2½fl oz) red wine**
**75ml (2½fl oz) hot vegetable stock**
**a small handful of freshly chopped**
**flat-leafed parsley**
**sea salt and freshly ground black**
**pepper**

**1.** Preheat the oven to 200°C (180°C fan oven) mark 6. Rub the potatoes with a little oil and put them on a baking tray. Scatter with sea salt and a pinch of smoked paprika and bake for 1–1½ hours.

**2.** Meanwhile, heat the 1 tbsp oil in a large pan. Add the shallots and fry over a low heat for 1–2 minutes until they start to soften.

**3.** Add the rosemary and the 1 tsp paprika and fry for 1–2 minutes, then add the beans, tomatoes, sugar, Worcestershire sauce, wine and hot stock. Season with salt and ground black pepper, then bring to the boil, reduce the heat and simmer, uncovered, for 10–15 minutes. Serve with the baked potatoes, scattered with parsley.

**GOES WELL WITH...**
*a sprinkle of grated Cheddar*

# Chicken Tagine

Preparation time 15 minutes • Cooking time 25 minutes • Serves 4 • Per Serving 260 calories, 8g fat (of which 2g saturates), 33g carbohydrates, 17g protein, 3g fibre, 0.2g salt

**1 tbsp vegetable oil**

**8 chicken drumsticks**

**½ tsp each ground cumin, coriander, cinnamon and paprika**

**75g (3oz) ready to eat dried apricots, finely chopped**

**40g (1½oz) raisins**

**400g can chopped tomatoes**

**75g (3oz) couscous**

**a large handful of fresh coriander, chopped**

**salt and freshly ground black pepper**

**1.** Heat the oil in a large heatproof casserole. Brown the drumsticks well all over. Stir in the spices and cook for 1 minute. Add the apricots, raisins, tomatoes, 400ml (13fl oz) water and some seasoning. Simmer for 10 minutes.

**2.** Stir in the couscous and simmer for a further 5 minutes or until the couscous is tender and the chicken is cooked through. Check the seasoning. Sprinkle with chopped coriander and serve immediately.

# Rabbit Ragu with Pappardelle

Preparation time 25 minutes • Cooking time about 1¼ hours • Serves 6 • Per Serving 280 calories, 7g fat (of which 2g saturates), 34g carbohydrates, 22g protein, 3g fibre, 0.8g salt

**450g (1lb) diced rabbit meat (ask your butcher or order via your supermarket)**
**1 tbsp plain flour**
**1 tbsp olive oil**
**1 onion, finely chopped**
**2 celery sticks, finely chopped**
**1 large carrot, finely chopped**
**2 rosemary sprigs**
**1 bay leaf**
**2 tbsp tomato purée**
**450ml (¾ pint) chicken stock**
**400g can chopped tomatoes**
**200g (7oz) dried pappardelle pasta**
**salt and freshly ground black pepper**

**1.** Dry the rabbit pieces roughly with kitchen paper and sprinkle over the flour. Heat the oil in a large pan, add the rabbit, onion, celery and carrot. Fry for 5 minutes, adding a little water if the pan gets dry.

**2.** Add the rosemary, bay leaf, tomato purée, stock, tomatoes and plenty of seasoning. Bring to the boil, reduce the heat, cover and simmer for 45 minutes. Take off the lid and simmer for a further 15 minutes, stirring occasionally.

**3.** When the rabbit has 15 minutes left to cook, bring a large pan of salted water to the boil and cook the pasta according to the pack instructions. Drain the pasta.

**4.** Check the seasoning of the ragu and serve immediately with pasta.

# Zingy Fish

Preparation time about 10 minutes • Cooking time 12 minutes • Serves 4 • Per Serving 228 calories, 7g fat (of which 1g saturates), 11g carbohydrates, 29g protein, 3g fibre, 0.5g salt

125g (4oz) tenderstem broccoli, halved lengthways

250g (9oz) fine asparagus

4 × 125g (4oz) skinless and boneless white fish fillets, such as haddock, pollock, cod or coley, ideally sustainably caught

50ml (2fl oz) white wine

1 orange, cut into 8 wedges

75g (3oz) sourdough bread, torn into pieces

2 tbsp olive oil

salt and freshly ground black pepper

1. Preheat the oven to 220°C (200°C fan) mark 7. Spread the broccoli and asparagus in an even layer in a medium roasting tin. Lay the fish fillets on top and pour over the wine. Tuck the orange wedges and bread around the fish. Drizzle over the olive oil and season well.

2. Cook in the oven for 10–12 minutes, or until the fish is cooked through and the vegetables are just tender (they should still have bite). Serve immediately.

GOES WELL WITH...
*boiled rice or salad*

# Crusted Cod with Minted Pea Mash

Preparation time 10 minutes • Cooking time about 15 minutes • Serves 4 • Per Serving 270 calories, 10g fat
(of which 3g saturates), 12g carbohydrates, 37g protein, 6g fibre, 0.5g salt

**50g (2oz) sun-dried tomatoes**

**2 tbsp sun-dried tomato oil taken
from the jar, plus extra to serve**

**25g (1oz) grated Parmesan**

**4 skinless cod fillets**

**500g (1lb 2oz) frozen peas**

**1 tbsp extra virgin olive oil**

**a small handful of freshly chopped
mint**

**salt and freshly ground black
pepper**

**1.** Preheat the oven to 200°C (180°C fan oven) mark 6. Put the sun-dried tomatoes, sun-dried tomato oil and Parmesan into a blender and whiz to make a thick paste. Alternatively, bash the ingredients together using a pestle and mortar.

**2.** Put the cod fillets on a non-stick baking tray and top each piece with a quarter of the tomato mixture. Roast in the oven for 12–15 minutes until the fish is cooked through and flakes easily when pushed with a knife.

**3.** Meanwhile, bring a medium pan of water to the boil and cook the peas for 3–4 minutes until tender. Drain. Put the peas into a food processor with the olive oil, mint and some seasoning. Whiz until the mixture is the consistency of a chunky mash. Serve immediately with the cod and a drizzle of the sun-dried tomato oil.

# Prawn & Pineapple Skewers

Preparation time 15 minutes • Cooking time about 10 minutes • Serves 4 • Per 3 Skewers 153 calories, 2g fat (of which 0.3g saturates), 19g carbohydrates, 14g protein, 2g fibre, 0.8g salt

**300g (11oz) raw peeled king prawns**
**400g (14oz) fresh pineapple chunks**
**2 red peppers, seeded and cut into 4cm (1½in) chunks**
**½ tbsp vegetable oil**
**grated zest and juice of 2 limes**
**1 tsp fish sauce**
**1 tbsp runny honey**
**2cm (¾in) piece fresh root ginger, peeled and grated**
**1 garlic clove, finely chopped**
**½–1 red chilli, to taste, seeded and finely chopped**
**freshly ground black pepper**

**1.** Soak 12 wooden skewers in hot water for 5 minutes. Preheat the grill to medium.

**2.** Divide the prawns, pineapple and pepper chunks among the presoaked skewers. Arrange the skewers on a baking sheet, brush with oil and grill for 3 minutes on each side or until the prawns have turned pink and the pineapple and peppers have just started to colour.

**3.** Stir the remaining ingredients (except the ground black pepper) together in a small bowl, then brush a little of the sauce over the cooked skewers. Season the skewers with pepper, then serve with the remaining sauce as a dip.

### GOES WELL WITH...
• *extra lime wedges to squeeze over the skewers*
• *boiled rice*

# Cheesy Polenta with Tomato Sauce

Preparation time 15 minutes • Cooking time about 40 minutes, plus cooling • Serves 6 • Per Serving 249 calories, 9g fat (of which 4g saturates), 31g carbohydrates, 10g protein, 1g fibre, 0.4g salt

a little vegetable oil

225g (8oz) polenta

4 tbsp freshly chopped herbs, such
   as oregano, chives and flat-
   leafed parsley

100g (3½oz) freshly grated
   Parmesan, plus a few extra
   Parmesan  shavings to serve

salt and freshly ground black
   pepper

**FOR THE TOMATO
AND BASIL SAUCE**

1 tbsp vegetable oil

3 garlic cloves, crushed

500g carton creamed tomatoes
   or passata

1 bay leaf

1 fresh thyme sprig

a large pinch of caster sugar

3 tbsp freshly chopped basil,
   plus extra to garnish

**1.** Lightly oil a 25.5 × 18cm (10 × 7in) dish. Bring 1.1 litres (2 pints) water and ¼ tsp salt to the boil in a large pan. Sprinkle in the polenta, whisking constantly. Reduce the heat and simmer, stirring frequently, for 10–15 minutes until the mixture leaves the sides of the pan.

**2.** Stir in the herbs and Parmesan and season to taste with salt and ground black pepper. Turn into the prepared dish and leave to cool.

**3.** Next, make the tomato and basil sauce. Heat the oil in a pan, add the garlic and fry for 30 seconds (do not brown). Add the creamed tomatoes or passata, the bay leaf, thyme and sugar. Season with salt and ground black pepper and bring to the boil, then reduce the heat and simmer, uncovered, for 5–10 minutes. Remove the bay leaf and thyme sprig and add the chopped basil.

**4.** To serve, preheat a griddle or grill. Cut the polenta into pieces and lightly brush with oil. Fry on the hot griddle for 3–4 minutes on each side, or under the hot grill for 7–8 minutes on each side. Serve with the tomato and basil sauce, and extra chopped basil and Parmesan shavings.

**GET AHEAD**
*Complete the recipe to the end of step 3. Cover and chill separately for up to two days.*

# Tomato Risotto

Preparation time 10 minutes • Cooking time about 30 minutes • Serves 6 • Per Serving 264 calories, 4g fat (of which 1g saturates), 49g carbohydrates, 4g protein, 1g fibre, 0.5g salt

**1 large rosemary sprig**
**2 tbsp olive oil**
**1 small onion, finely chopped**
**350g (12oz) risotto (arborio) rice**
**4 tbsp dry white wine**
**750ml (1¼ pints) hot vegetable stock**
**300g (11oz) cherry tomatoes, halved**
**salt and freshly ground black pepper**

**1.** Pull the leaves from the rosemary and chop roughly. Put to one side.

**2.** Heat the olive oil in a flameproof casserole, add the onion and cook for 8–10 minutes until beginning to soften. Add the rice and stir to coat in the oil and onion. Pour in the wine, then the hot stock, stirring well to mix.

**3.** Bring to the boil, stirring, then reduce the heat, cover and simmer for 5 minutes. Stir in the tomatoes and chopped rosemary. Simmer, covered, for a further 10–15 minutes until the rice is tender and most of the liquid has been absorbed. Season to taste with salt and ground black pepper and serve immediately.

**GOES WELL WITH...**
*a sprinkle of Parmesan shavings*
*green salad*

# Vegetable Frittata

Preparation time 15 minutes • Cooking time 25 minutes • Serves 4 • Per Serving 236 calories, 17g fat (of which 7g saturates), 6g carbohydrates, 16g protein, 3g fibre, 0.6g salt

**15g (½oz) butter**

**1 red onion, finely sliced**

**2 green peppers, seeded and finely sliced**

**200g (7oz) cherry tomatoes**

**8 medium eggs**

**2 tbsp fresh chopped mint**

**25g (1oz) mature Cheddar, grated**

**salt and freshly ground black pepper**

**1.** Melt the butter in a 23cm (9in) pan (suitable for use under the grill). Add the onion and peppers and gently fry for 10 minutes, adding a splash of water if the pan looks a little dry. Add the cherry tomatoes and fry for 2–3 minutes.

**2.** Preheat the grill to medium. In a large bowl, beat together the eggs and most of the mint. Season well with salt and ground black pepper. Pour the egg mixture into the frying pan and use a wooden spoon to spread the mixture evenly between the vegetables. Cook on the hob over a low heat for 5 minutes until the egg is set around the edges.

**3.** Sprinkle over the grated cheese. Grill for 5 minutes or until the egg is cooked and the cheese is golden and bubbling. Sprinkle with the remaining mint, cut the frittata into wedges and serve hot or at room temperature.

**GOES WELL WITH...**
*green salad*

# Cheat's Chocolate Soufflés

Preparation time 15 minutes • Cooking time about 12 minutes • Serves 6 • Per Serving 126 calories, 5g fat (of which 2g saturates), 19g carbohydrates, 3g protein, 0.4g fibre, 0.1g salt

**butter to grease**
**75g (3oz) plain chocolate**
**225ml (8fl oz) fresh chocolate custard**
**3 medium egg whites**
**25g (1oz) caster sugar**
**icing sugar to dust**

1. Preheat the oven to 220°C (200°C fan oven) mark 7. Put a baking sheet on the middle shelf to heat up, making sure there's enough space for the soufflés to rise. Grease six 125ml (4fl oz) ramekins.

2. Finely grate the chocolate, or whiz until it resembles breadcrumbs. Dust the insides of the ramekins with 25g (1oz) of the chocolate.

3. Mix the custard and remaining chocolate together in a large bowl. In a separate bowl, whisk the egg whites until stiff but not dry, then gradually add the caster sugar to the egg whites, whisking well after each addition. Using a metal spoon, fold the egg whites into the custard mixture.

4. Quickly divide the mixture among the prepared ramekins, put them on to the preheated baking sheet and bake for 10–12 minutes until well risen. Dust the soufflés with icing sugar and serve immediately.

# Summer Pudding

Preparation time 10 minutes • Cooking time 10 minutes, plus overnight chilling • Serves 8 • Per Serving 204 calories, 1g fat (of which trace saturates), 46g carbohydrates, 5g protein, 5g fibre, 0.4g salt

**800g (1lb 12oz) mixed summer berries, such as 250g (9oz) each redcurrants and blackcurrants and 300g (11oz) raspberries**
**125g (4oz) golden caster sugar**
**3 tbsp crème de cassis**
**9 thick slices slightly stale white bread, crusts removed**

**1.** Put the redcurrants and blackcurrants into a medium pan. Add the sugar and cassis and bring to a simmer. Cook for 3–5 minutes until the sugar has dissolved. Add the raspberries and cook for 2 minutes. Once the fruit is cooked, taste it – there should be a good balance between tart and sweet.

**2.** Meanwhile, line a 1 litre (1¾ pint) bowl with clingfilm. Put the base of the bowl on one piece of bread and cut around it. Put the circle of bread in the bottom of the bowl.

**3.** Line the inside of the bowl with more slices of bread, slightly overlapping them to prevent any gaps. Spoon in the fruit, making sure the juice soaks into the bread. Keep back a few spoonfuls of juice in case the bread is unevenly soaked when you turn out the pudding.

**4.** Cut the remaining bread to fit the top of the pudding neatly, using a sharp knife to trim any excess bread from around the edges. Wrap in clingfilm, weigh down with a saucer and a can and chill overnight.

**5.** To serve, unwrap the outer clingfilm, upturn the pudding on to a plate and remove the inner clingfilm. Drizzle with the reserved juice and serve.

**GOES WELL WITH...**
*a dollop of low-fat crème fraîche*

# Apple & Blueberry Strudel

Preparation time 15 minutes • Cooking time 40 minutes • Serves 6 • Per Serving 287 calories, 2g fat (of which trace saturates), 60g carbohydrates, 1g protein, 2g fibre, 0.1g salt

**700g (1½lb) red apples, quartered, cored and thickly sliced**
**1 tbsp lemon juice**
**2 tbsp golden caster sugar**
**100g (3½oz) dried blueberries**
**1 tbsp olive oil**
**6 sheets of filo pastry, thawed if frozen**

**1.** Preheat the oven to 190°C (170°C fan oven) mark 5. Put the apples into a bowl and mix with the lemon juice, 1 tbsp of the sugar and the blueberries.

**2.** Warm the oil. Lay three sheets of filo pastry side by side, overlapping the long edges. Brush with the oil. Cover with three more sheets of filo and brush again.

**3.** Tip the apple mixture on to the pastry and roll up from a long edge. Put on to a non-stick baking sheet. Brush with the remaining oil and sprinkle with the remaining

sugar. Bake for 40 minutes or until the pastry is golden and the apples soft. Serve.

**GOES WELL WITH...**
*a dollop of low-fat yogurt*

**HEALTHY TIP**
*This dessert is low in fat, as it is made with filo pastry (which contains virtually no fat) instead of shortcrust pastry (around 30g per 100g/3½oz). The blueberries are rich in anthocyanins – the pigment that gives berries their intense colour – which can help to prevent cancer and heart disease. Apples provide good levels of vitamin C and fibre.*

# Baked Apricots with Almonds

Preparation time 5 minutes • Cooking time about 25 minutes • Serves 6 • Per Serving 124 calories, 6g fat (of which 2g saturates), 16g carbohydrates, 2g protein, 2g fibre, 0.1g salt

**12 apricots, halved and stoned**
**3 tbsp golden caster sugar**
**2 tbsp amaretto liqueur**
**25g (1oz) unsalted butter**
**25g (1oz) flaked almonds**

**1.** Preheat the oven to 200°C (180°C fan oven) mark 6. Put the apricot halves, cut side up, in an ovenproof dish. Sprinkle with the sugar, drizzle with the liqueur, then dot each apricot half with a little butter. Scatter the flaked almonds over them.

**2.** Bake in the oven for 20–25 minutes until the apricots are soft and the juices are syrupy. Serve warm.

**GOES WELL WITH...**
*a dollop of low-fat crème fraîche*

# Apple Compote

Preparation time 10 minutes, plus chilling • Cooking time 5 minutes • Serves 2 • Per Serving 188 calories, 7g fat (of which 1g saturates), 29g carbohydrates, 4g protein, 3g fibre, 0g salt

**250g (9oz) cooking apples, peeled and chopped**
**juice of ½ lemon**
**1 tbsp golden caster sugar**
**a pinch of ground cinnamon**
**25g (1oz) raisins**
**25g (1oz) chopped almonds**
**1 tbsp low-fat natural yogurt**

**1.** Put the apples into a pan with the lemon juice, sugar and 2 tbsp cold water. Cook gently for 5 minutes or until soft. Transfer to a bowl.

**2.** Sprinkle a little cinnamon over the top, then cool and chill. It will keep for up to three days.

**3.** Serve with the raisins, chopped almonds and yogurt.

**COOK'S TIP**
*To microwave, put the apples, lemon juice, sugar and water into a microwave-proof bowl, cover loosely with clingfilm and cook on full power in an 850W microwave oven for 4 minutes or until the apples are just soft.*

# Raspberry & Elderflower Jelly

Preparation time 20 minutes, plus chilling • Cooking time about 10 minutes, plus cooling • Serves 8
Per Serving 61 calories, 0g fat, 13g carbohydrates, 3g protein, 1g fibre, 0.1g salt

**8 sheets leaf gelatine**
**100ml (3½fl oz) elderflower cordial**
**500g (1lb 2oz) raspberries**
**75g (3oz) caster sugar**

1. Wet a 900g (2lb) loaf tin, then line it neatly with clingfilm and put to one side. For the elderflower jelly, soak four of the gelatine sheets in cold water for 5 minutes to soften them. Meanwhile, put the cordial in a pan with 100ml (3½fl oz) water and heat until steaming, but not boiling. Take off the heat. Squeeze out the excess water from the gelatine, then add the softened sheets to the elderflower mixture and stir until dissolved. Pour the mixture into a jug, stir in 200ml (7fl oz) cold water and leave to cool completely. When cool, tip into the prepared loaf tin and evenly scatter 100g (3½oz) of the raspberries over. Chill for 2 hours or until just set.

2. While the elderflower jelly is chilling, make the raspberry jelly. Soak the remaining gelatine sheets in cold water as before. Put the remaining raspberries in a pan with 250ml (9fl oz) water and the sugar. Heat gently until the sugar has dissolved, then bring the mixture to the boil and bubble for 5 minutes, mashing the fruit as you stir until it's completely broken down and the mixture is fragrant. Strain through a fine sieve into a clean pan. Squeeze out the excess water from the gelatine, add to the raspberry mixture and heat gently, stirring until dissolved. Leave to cool completely.

3. Carefully pour the cooled raspberry jelly into the loaf tin over the just-set elderflower layer. Chill the jelly again until completely set – about 5 hours. When ready to serve, carefully invert the jelly on to a serving plate to unmould it. Peel off the clingfilm and serve in slices.

# Lemon Sorbet

Preparation time 10 minutes, plus chilling and freezing • Cooking time 15 minutes, plus cooling • Serves 4
Per Serving 127 calories, 0g fat, 33g carbohydrates, 1g protein, 0g fibre, 0.1g salt

**3 juicy lemons**
**125g (4oz) golden caster sugar**
**1 large egg white**

1. Finely pare the lemon zest, using a zester, then squeeze the juice and set aside. Put the zest into a pan with the sugar and 350ml (12fl oz) water and heat gently until the sugar has dissolved. Increase the heat and boil for 10 minutes. Leave to cool.

2. Stir the lemon juice into the cooled sugar syrup. Cover and chill in the fridge for 30 minutes.

3. Strain the syrup through a fine sieve into a bowl. In another bowl, beat the egg white until just frothy, then whisk into the lemon mixture.

4. For best results, freeze in an ice-cream maker. (Alternatively, pour into a shallow freezerproof container and freeze until almost frozen; mash well with a fork and freeze until solid.) Transfer the sorbet to the fridge 30 minutes before serving to soften slightly.

# Three-ingredient Strawberry Ice Cream

Preparation time 10 minutes • Serves 6 • Per Serving 175 calories, 11g fat (of which 7g saturates), 18g carbohydrates, 1g protein, 0.9g fibre, 0g salt

**500g (1lb 2oz) hulled and frozen strawberries**
**75g (3oz) icing sugar**
**125ml (4fl oz) double cream**

**1.** Put all the ingredients into a food processor. Pulse until the strawberries are fairly broken down, then whiz until the mixture is smooth.

**2.** Serve immediately or transfer to a freezerproof container and freeze for up to one month. Allow the ice cream to soften a little at room temperature before serving.

**GET AHEAD**
*Make in advance and keep well wrapped in the freezer for up to two weeks.*

# UNDER 400
# CALORIES

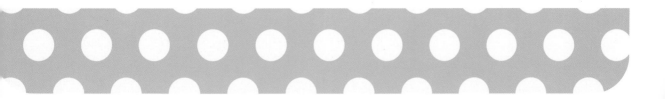

# Toasted Oats with Berries

Preparation time 10 minutes • Cooking time about 10 minutes, plus cooling • Serves 4 • Per Serving 327 calories, 15g fat (of which 3g saturates), 44g carbohydrates, 8g protein, 5g fibre, 0.1g salt

25g (1oz) hazelnuts, roughly
  chopped
125g (4oz) rolled oats
1 tbsp olive oil
125g (4oz) strawberries, sliced
250g (9oz) blueberries
200g (7oz) Greek yogurt
2 tbsp runny honey

1. Preheat the grill to medium. Put the hazelnuts into a bowl with the oats. Drizzle with the oil and mix well, then spread out on a baking sheet. Toast the oat mixture for 5–10 minutes until it starts to crisp up. Remove from the heat and leave to cool.

2. Put the strawberries into a large bowl with the blueberries and yogurt. Stir in the oats and hazelnuts, drizzle with the honey and divide among four dishes. Serve immediately.

**TRY SOMETHING DIFFERENT**
*If you don't have any strawberries or blueberries to hand, substitute with other fruits, such as raspberries.*

# Beans on Toast

Preparation time 5 minutes • Cooking time about 15 minutes • Serves 4 • Per Serving 364 calories, 9g fat
(of which 2g saturates), 55g carbohydrates, 15g protein, 8g fibre, 2.1g salt

**1 tbsp olive oil**
**2 garlic cloves, finely sliced**
**400g can borlotti or cannellini beans, drained and rinsed**
**400g can chickpeas, drained and rinsed**
**400g can chopped tomatoes**
**2 fresh rosemary sprigs**
**4 slices sourdough or Granary bread**
**25g (1oz) Parmesan**

**1.** Heat the oil in a pan over a low heat, add the garlic and cook for 1 minute, stirring gently.

**2.** Add the beans and chickpeas to the pan with the tomatoes and bring to the boil. Strip the leaves from the rosemary, then chop finely and add to the pan. Reduce the heat and simmer for 8–10 minutes until thickened.

**3.** Meanwhile, toast the bread and put on to plates. Grate the Parmesan into the bean mixture, stir once, then spoon over the bread. Serve immediately.

**HEALTHY TIP**
*This low-GI breakfast will give you energy through until lunchtime.*

# Sunday Brunch Bake

Preparation time 15 minutes • Cooking time about 35 minutes • Serves 6 • Per Serving 330 calories, 16g fat (of which 6g saturates), 26g carbohydrates, 20g protein, 2g fibre, 1.9g salt

**butter, to grease**
**6 English muffins**
**1½–2 tbsp wholegrain mustard**
**6 streaky bacon rashers**
**12 raw cocktail sausages**
**600ml (1 pint) semi-skimmed milk**
**4 large eggs**
**2 tbsp chives, freshly chopped,**
  **plus extra to garnish**
**40g (1½oz) mature Cheddar**
  **cheese, grated**
**a large handful of cherry tomatoes**
**salt and freshly ground black**
  **pepper**

1. Preheat oven to 200°C (180°C fan oven) mark 6. Grease an ovenproof rectangular dish roughly 22cm × 33cm (8.5in × 13in) and set aside.

2. Split the muffins in half horizontally and spread the cut sides with mustard. Next, cut the bacon rashers in half to make two shorter pieces. Arrange the muffins (cut side up) and bacon in the dish, then dot around the sausages.

3. In a large jug, mix together the milk, eggs, chives and some seasoning. Pour the mixture over the muffins, then scatter over the grated cheese and cherry tomatoes.

4. Bake for 30–35 minutes or until the sausages are golden and the liquid has set. Garnish with chives and serve immediately.

**GOES WELL WITH...**
*baked beans*

# Pea & Ham Soup

Preparation time 10 minutes • Cooking time about 15 minutes • Serves 4 • Per Serving 323 calories, 14g fat (of which 5g saturates), 19g carbohydrates, 30g protein, 13g fibre, 3g salt

**1 tbsp oil**
**1 onion, chopped**
**750g (1lb 11oz) frozen peas**
**1 litre (1¾ pints) chicken stock**
**2 x 200g (7oz) unsmoked gammon**
   **steaks, trimmed of fat**
**1 tbsp freshly chopped chives,**
   **plus extra to garnish**
**4 tsp half-fat crème fraîche**
**salt and freshly ground black**
   **pepper**

**1.** Heat the oil in a large pan and fry the onion for 10 minutes until softened but not coloured.

**2.** Stir in the peas and chicken stock and bring to the boil. Add the gammon steaks and simmer for 5 minutes until cooked through.

**3.** Lift out the gammon and set aside on a board. Blend the soup until completely smooth (do this in batches, if necessary). Meanwhile, shred the gammon into fine pieces, discarding any fat.

**4.** Return the soup to the pan, reheat, and add the shredded gammon and chives. Check the seasoning. Divide among four warmed soup bowls and serve garnished with the crème fraîche, extra chives and ground black pepper.

**GOES WELL WITH...**
*crusty bread*

# Beef Pho

Preparation time 15 minutes • Cooking time about 25 minutes • Serves 4 • Per Serving 331 calories, 8g fat (of which 2g saturates), 37g carbohydrates, 28g protein, 1g fibre, 2g salt

1 tbsp vegetable oil

400g (14oz) sirloin steak, excess fat trimmed

1.6 litres (2¾ pints) beef stock

1 star anise

4 whole cloves

1 cinnamon stick

1 tbsp each soy and fish sauce, plus extra to taste

150g (5oz) rice noodles

1 onion, very thinly sliced

225g (8oz) bean sprouts

1 red chilli, seeded and sliced into rings

a small handful each of fresh basil and coriander, chopped

salt and freshly ground black pepper

1. Heat the oil in a large frying pan over a high heat. Pat the steak dry with kitchen paper, season well and fry for 5–6 minutes, turning once, for medium meat (cook for shorter/longer if you prefer). Lift the steaks out of the frying pan and put to one side on a board.

2. Pour the stock into a separate large pan, add the spices and bring to the boil, then reduce the heat and simmer for 5 minutes. Add the soy sauce, fish sauce and noodles and cook for 5 minutes, then add the onion, bean sprouts and chilli. Take off the heat.

3. Slice the steak into thin strips. Divide the soup among four large bowls. Add a quarter of the beef strips to each bowl, sprinkle with the herbs and serve.

GOES WELL WITH...
*lime wedges to squeeze over the soup*

# Goulash Soup

Preparation time 20 minutes • Cooking time about 2½ hours • Serves 6 • Per Serving 343 calories, 14g fat (of which 7g saturates), 22g carbohydrates, 33g protein, 4g fibre, 0.8g salt

**700g (1½lb) silverside or lean chuck steak**
**25g (1oz) butter**
**225g (8oz) onions, chopped**
**1 small green pepper, seeded and chopped**
**4 tomatoes, skinned and quartered**
**150g (5oz) tomato purée**
**600ml (1 pint) rich beef stock**
**1 tbsp paprika**
**450g (1lb) potatoes**
**150ml (¼ pint) soured cream**
**salt and freshly ground black pepper**

1. Remove any excess fat or gristle and cut the meat into small pieces. Season well with 2 tsp salt and ground black pepper to taste.

2. Melt the butter in a large pan, add the onions and green pepper and sauté until tender.

3. Add the meat pieces, tomatoes, tomato purée, stock and paprika. Stir well and bring to the boil, then reduce the heat, cover the pan and simmer for 2½ hours, stirring occasionally.

4. Half an hour before the end of cooking, peel and cut the potatoes into bite-size pieces, bring to the boil in lightly salted water, reduce the heat and simmer until cooked. Drain well and add to the soup.

5. Check the seasoning and stir in 2 tbsp soured cream. Ladle into warmed bowls and serve the remaining soured cream separately, for each person to spoon into their soup.

# Red Lentil Soup with Low-fat Corn Bread

Preparation time 30 minutes • Cooking time about 30 minutes • Serves 4 • Per Serving (with 1 slice of cornbread) 359 calories, 4g fat (of which 1g saturates), 64g carbohydrates, 25g protein, 6g fibre, 0.5g salt

1 tsp extra virgin olive oil,
   plus extra to drizzle
1 onion, roughly chopped
2 celery sticks, roughly chopped
1 garlic clove, chopped
1 tsp chilli powder (or to taste)
250g (9oz) red lentils, washed
400g can chopped tomatoes
1.1 litres (2 pints) vegetable stock

**FOR THE CORNBREAD**
(cuts into 8 slices)
100g (3½oz) plain flour
100g (3½oz) quick-cook polenta
1 tbsp caster sugar
½ tsp bicarbonate of soda
1 medium egg
175g (6oz) low-fat natural yogurt
salt

1. Start by making the soup. Heat the oil in a large pan. Add the onion and celery and gently cook for 10 minutes until softened. Stir in the garlic and chilli powder and cook for 1 minute. Add the lentils, tomatoes and stock and bring to the boil, then reduce the heat and simmer gently for 15 minutes or until the lentils are tender.

2. Meanwhile, make the cornbread. Preheat the oven to 180°C (160°C fan oven) mark 4 and line a 450g (1lb) loaf tin with baking parchment. Measure the flour, polenta, sugar and soda into a large bowl. Add ½–¾ tsp salt (depending on taste) and whisk to combine.

3. In a separate jug, whisk together the egg and yogurt. Add to the dry ingredients and whisk until just combined. Scrape into the prepared tin, level the surface and bake for 20–25 minutes until golden and firm to the touch. Leave to rest in the tin for 10 minutes.

4. Blend the soup until smooth (do this in batches if necessary) and pour back into the pan. Check the seasoning (if the soup is too thick for your liking, add a little more water).

5. To serve, reheat the soup (if necessary), then ladle into warmed bowls and drizzle with a little extra oil. Serve with the warm sliced cornbread.

# Harissa Chicken & Couscous Salad

Preparation time 15 minutes • Cooking time about 25 minutes • Serves 4 • Per Serving 346 calories, 7g fat (of which 3g saturates), 28g carbohydrates, 44g protein, 0.4g fibre, 3g salt

1 tbsp rose harissa paste
4 skinless chicken breasts
1 litre (1¾ pints) chicken stock
200g (7oz) giant wholewheat
   couscous
½ courgette, finely chopped
100g (3½oz) cherry tomatoes,
   quartered
2 spring onions, finely sliced
40g (1½oz) feta, crumbled
a large handful of fresh coriander
   leaves, roughly chopped
salt and freshly ground black
   pepper

1. Preheat the oven to 200°C (180°C fan oven) mark 6. Rub the harissa paste over the chicken breasts and put them on a baking tray. Roast for 20–25 minutes until cooked through.

2. Meanwhile, bring the stock to the boil in a large pan. Add the couscous and simmer according to the pack instructions or until tender – about 8 minutes. Drain.

3. Transfer the couscous to a large platter, add the courgette, tomatoes, onions, feta, coriander and some seasoning and mix through.

4. Carefully slice the cooked chicken and lay on top of the couscous salad. Serve warm or at room temperature.

GOES WELL WITH...
*a drizzle of tzatziki*

# Smoked Mackerel Superfood Salad

Preparation time 15 minutes • Serves 4 • Per Serving 358 calories, 21g fat (of which 4g saturates), 22g carbohydrates, 21g protein, 7g fibre, 1g salt

1 red grapefruit

½–1 tbsp wholegrain mustard, to taste

1 tbsp rapeseed oil

175g (6oz) smoked mackerel, skinned and flaked

300g (11oz) raw tenderstem broccoli, thinly sliced lengthways

400g can lentils, drained and rinsed

100g (3½oz) pomegranate seeds

100g bag watercress

25g (1oz) pumpkin seeds

salt and freshly ground black pepper

1. Slice the top and bottom off the grapefruit and sit it on a board. Using a small serrated knife, cut away the peel and white pith. Hold the grapefruit over a small bowl and cut between the membranes to separate the segments. Squeeze the membranes into a separate small bowl to extract as much juice as possible (add any extra juice from the segment bowl).

2. Whisk the mustard, oil and plenty of seasoning into the juice bowl to make a dressing.

3. Put all the remaining ingredients into a large bowl and toss together. Drizzle the dressing over and add the grapefruit segments. Toss carefully together and serve.

# Grilled Avocado, Tomato & Mozzarella Salad

Preparation time 20 minutes, plus standing • Cooking time about 10 minutes • Serves 4 • Per Serving
371 calories, 31g fat (of which 12g saturates), 9g carbohydrates, 15g protein, 5g fibre, 0.7g salt

**1kg (2lb 2oz) mixed tomatoes**
**2 ripe avocados, but not overly soft**
**1 tbsp extra virgin olive oil**
**2 × 125g (4oz) balls buffalo**
  **mozzarella, drained**
**a punnet of cress or a large handful**
  **of Greek basil**
**balsamic vinegar to drizzle**
**salt and freshly ground black**
  **pepper**

**1.** Start by preparing the tomatoes. To add interest to your salad, chop all the tomatoes differently – halve or quarter smaller ones, slice or roughly chop larger ones. Put all the tomatoes into a colander and sprinkle with ½ tsp salt, then toss together and leave in the sink for 20 minutes – this will help any excess, flavourless moisture drain out of the tomatoes.

**2.** Meanwhile, halve, stone and peel the avocados. Slice the flesh into 1cm (½in) thick slices. Preheat a griddle pan over a high heat.

Brush the avocado slices with the oil and arrange neatly on the griddle. Leave in place until charred black lines appear on the underside of the slices, then flip over and repeat on the other side.

**3.** To serve, tip the tomatoes on to a large flat platter. Rip the mozzarella into bite-size pieces and dot among the tomatoes. Snip the cress over or sprinkle with basil. Season with ground black pepper and drizzle with some balsamic vinegar.

**HEALTHY TIP**
*Tomatoes are full of vitamin C, which is a powerful antioxidant and antiviral nutrient crucial for a healthy immune system.*

# Greek Pasta Salad

Preparation time 10 minutes • Cooking time 20 minutes • Serves 2 • Per Serving 382 calories, 27g fat (of which 8g saturates), 25g carbohydrates, 9g protein, 3g fibre, 2.5g salt

**3 tbsp olive oil**

**2 tbsp lemon juice**

**150g (5oz) cooked pasta shapes, cooled**

**75g (3oz) feta, crumbled**

**3 tomatoes, roughly chopped**

**2 tbsp small pitted black olives**

**½ cucumber, roughly chopped**

**1 small red onion, finely sliced**

**salt and freshly ground black pepper**

**a handful of freshly chopped parsley**

**lemon zest to garnish**

**1.** Mix the oil and lemon juice together in a salad bowl, then add the pasta, feta, tomatoes, olives, cucumber and onion. Season to taste with salt and ground black pepper, then stir to mix.

**2.** Sprinkle with parsley and lemon zest and serve.

# White Bean Salad

Preparation time 15 minutes • Serves 4 • Per Serving 346 calories, 13g fat (of which 5g saturates), 40g carbohydrates, 9g protein, 9g fibre, 2.2g salt

½ tbsp red wine vinegar

2 tbsp extra virgin olive oil

½ red cabbage

2 courgettes

410g can cannellini beans, drained and rinsed

410g can butter beans, drained and rinsed

½ red onion, finely chopped

100g (3½oz) stale unsliced bread, torn into small chunks

125g ball low-fat mozzarella, torn into small pieces

a handful of fresh basil leaves, chopped

salt and freshly ground black pepper

**1.** Whisk together the vinegar, oil, plenty of seasoning and a splash of water in a small bowl to make a dressing.

**2.** Cut out and discard the tough core from the cabbage, then finely shred the leaves and put into a large serving bowl. Using a y-shaped peeler, peel the courgettes into ribbons and add to the cabbage bowl. Add the remaining ingredients and dressing. Toss well to combine and serve.

# Mexican Chicken Stew

Preparation time 15 minutes • Cooking time about 30 minutes • Serves 4 • Per Serving 375 calories, 8g fat (of which 2g saturates), 41g carbohydrates, 36g protein, 5g fibre, 2g salt

**1 tbsp olive oil**

**1 onion, finely sliced**

**3 skinless chicken breasts, cut into finger-sized strips**

**1 green pepper, seeded and diced**

**1–1½ tsp chipotle paste, to taste (see Cook's Tip)**

**1 litre (1¾ pints) chicken stock**

**100g (3½oz) easy-cook rice, washed**

**410g can black-eyed beans, drained and rinsed**

**a large handful of fresh coriander, roughly chopped**

**salt and freshly ground black pepper**

**1.** Heat the oil in a large pan and fry the onion gently for 10 minutes or until softened. Add the chicken and green pepper and continue to fry for 5 minutes. Stir in the chipotle paste, stock and rice.

**2.** Bring the mixture to the boil, then reduce the heat and simmer for 15 minutes or until the rice is tender. Stir in the beans and most of the coriander. Check the seasoning.

**3.** Divide the soup among four bowls, garnish with the remaining coriander and serve.

**GOES WELL WITH…**

*a dollop of low-fat soured cream and low-fat guacamole (to stir through)*

**COOK'S TIP**

*The chipotle paste adds wonderful smokiness to this easy and filling stew. If you have trouble finding it, substitute with a seeded and finely chopped green chilli.*

# Cheesy Chicken Cobbler

Preparation time 20 minutes • Cooking time about 20 minutes • Serves 4 • Per Serving 372 calories, 12g fat (of which 4g saturates), 42g carbohydrates, 27g protein, 2g fibre, 1.7g salt

**200g (7oz) cooked skinless chicken breast, cut into bite-sized pieces**
**200g (7oz) frozen mixed vegetables**
**300g tin of tomato soup**
**175g (6oz) self-raising flour, plus extra to dust**
**½ tbsp baking powder**
**50g (2oz) mature Cheddar cheese, grated**
**75ml (3fl oz) semi-skimmed milk, plus extra to brush**
**1 medium egg, lightly beaten**
**½ tbsp vegetable oil**
**salt and freshly ground black pepper**

**1.** Preheat the oven to 200°C (180°C fan) mark 6. In a medium bowl, stir together the cooked chicken, frozen vegetables, soup and some seasoning. Pour the mixture into a rough 1 litre (1¾ pint) shallow ovenproof dish and set aside.

**2.** Sift the flour, baking powder and a large pinch of salt into a large bowl. Stir in most of the cheese. Beat the milk, egg and oil together in a separate bowl.

**3.** Pour the milk mixture into the flour bowl and use a cutlery knife to bring it together until the dough forms clumps. Add a splash of milk if it looks too dry.

**4.** Tip the dough on to a lightly floured surface and pat it into a rough 9 x 15cm (3½ x 6in) rectangle. Cut the rectangle into eight equal squares, then arrange the scones on top of the chicken mixture. Brush each scone with a little milk, then sprinkle over the remaining cheese.

**5.** Cook in the oven for 20 minutes or until the scones are risen and golden, and the filling is bubbling and piping hot. Serve immediately.

# Chicken Tarragon Sweet Potatoes

Preparation time 15 minutes • Cooking time about 40 minutes • Serves 4 • Per Serving 363 calories, 7g fat (of which 2g saturates), 54g carbohydrates, 25g protein, 6g fibre, 1g salt

**1 tbsp vegetable oil, plus extra for potatoes**
**4 large sweet potatoes**
**1 tbsp plain flour**
**250ml (8fl oz) semi-skimmed milk**
**½ tbsp wholegrain mustard**
**2 skinless cooked chicken breasts, sliced**
**1 fresh tarragon sprig, finely chopped, plus extra to garnish**
**50g (2oz) baby spinach leaves**
**salt and freshly ground black pepper**

**1.** Preheat the oven to 220°C (200°C fan oven) mark 7. Rub a little oil over the sweet potatoes, then put them on a baking tray and cook for 35–40 minutes until cooked (a knife should go through a potato easily).

**2.** About 10 minutes before the end of the potato cooking time, make the chicken sauce. Heat the oil in a small pan over a medium heat, then stir in the flour and cook for 1 minute. Remove from the heat and gradually whisk in the milk until smooth. Put back on the heat and bring to the boil, whisking all the time. Reduce the heat and simmer the sauce for 3 minutes, then whisk in the mustard and add the chicken. Cook for 2–3 minutes until the chicken is piping hot, then stir in the tarragon and spinach. Check the seasoning.

**3.** Take the sweet potatoes out of the oven and split them lengthways. Pull the halves gently apart, divide the filling equally among the potatoes and serve.

**GOES WELL WITH...**
*green vegetables or salad*

# Pork Escalopes & Apple Slaw

Preparation time 20 minutes • Cooking time about 5 minutes • Serves 4 • Per Serving 365 calories, 13g fat (of which 3g saturates), 34g carbohydrates, 31g protein, 2g fibre, 0.7g salt

**200g (7oz) 0% fat Greek yogurt**
**juice of 1 lemon**
**1 tsp wholegrain mustard**
**2 eating apples (skin on), cut into matchsticks**
**½ small red cabbage, finely shredded**
**a small handful of fresh parsley, chopped**
**75g (3oz) Rice Krispies**
**25g (1oz) plain flour**
**2 medium eggs, beaten**
**4 pork escalopes**
**2 tbsp sunflower oil**
**salt and freshly ground black pepper**

1. Put the yogurt, lemon juice and mustard into a large serving bowl and mix together. Stir in the apple matchsticks, cabbage and parsley. Check the seasoning and put to one side.

2. Whiz the Rice Krispies in a food processor until finely crushed. Tip on to a lipped plate. Put the flour and eggs on two separate lipped plates.

3. Dip each escalope into the flour to coat, tapping off any excess, then dip into the beaten eggs, followed by the cereal crumbs. Finish by dipping each escalope once more into the eggs before coating with a final layer of cereal.

4. Heat the oil in a large non-stick frying pan over a medium heat. Add the escalopes and fry for 5 minutes, turning once, until golden and cooked through. Serve with the apple slaw.

**GOES WELL WITH...**
*boiled new potatoes*

# Sausage & Gnocchi One-pan

Preparation time 20 minutes • Cooking time about 25 minutes • Serves 4 • Per Serving 306 calories, 8g fat
(of which 2g saturates), 44g carbohydrates, 13g protein, 10g fibre, 2.3g salt

1 tsp vegetable oil
2 large pork sausages
1 red onion, finely sliced
1 fat garlic clove, crushed
150g (5oz) gnocchi
2 × 410g cans cannellini beans,
    drained and rinsed
400ml (14fl oz) chicken stock
a large handful of baby spinach
    leaves or fresh parsley
salt and freshly ground black
    pepper

1. Heat the oil in a large, deep frying pan and fry the sausages and onion until golden.

2. Stir in the garlic, gnocchi, cannellini beans, stock and plenty of seasoning. Bring to the boil, then reduce the heat and simmer for 10–15 minutes until the sausages are cooked through.

3. Lift the sausages out of the mixture and slice into 1cm (½in) thick slices. Return the slices to the pan and fold the spinach or parsley through. Check the seasoning and serve.

**GOES WELL WITH...**
*crusty bread*

**HEALTHY TIP**
*You can still enjoy higher-fat ingredients, like sausages, but make them go further by bulking the dish up with healthier alternatives.*

# Salmon & Bulgur Wheat Pilau

Preparation time 5 minutes • Cooking time 20 minutes • Serves 4 • Per Serving 392 calories, 11g fat (of which 2g saturates), 40g carbohydrates, 33g protein, 5g fibre, 2g salt

1 tbsp olive oil

1 onion, chopped

175g (6oz) bulgur wheat

450ml (¾ pint) vegetable stock

400g can pink salmon, drained and flaked

125g (4oz) spinach, roughly chopped

225g (8oz) frozen peas

zest and juice of 1 lemon

salt and freshly ground black pepper

1. Heat the oil in a large pan. Add the onion and cook until softened. Stir in the bulgur wheat to coat in the oil, then stir in the stock and bring to the boil. Cover the pan, reduce the heat and simmer for 10–15 minutes until the stock has been fully absorbed.

2. Stir in the salmon, spinach, peas and lemon juice and cook until the spinach has wilted and the salmon and peas are heated through. Season with salt and ground black pepper and sprinkle with lemon zest before serving.

# Cajun Fish Wraps

Preparation time 15 minutes • Cooking time about 5 minutes • Serves 4 • Per Serving 303 calories, 10g fat (of which 2g saturates), 3.5g fibre, 32g carbohydrates, 23g protein, 0.7g salt

**zest and juice of ½ lime**
**4 tbsp natural yogurt**
**1 tbsp freshly chopped chives**
**25g (1oz) dry polenta**
**1 tbsp cajun spice**
**375g (13oz) white fish fillets, such**
    **as plaice, cod or pollock, cut into**
    **finger-size strips**
**oil to brush**
**50g (2oz) rocket leaves**
**1 avocado, stoned and cut into**
    **strips**
**1 red pepper, seeded and cut into**
    **strips**
**4 flour tortillas**
**salt and freshly ground black**
    **pepper**

1. In a bowl, mix together the lime zest and juice, yogurt, chives and some seasoning. Put to one side.

2. Preheat the grill to high. In a medium bowl, mix together the polenta, cajun spice and a little seasoning. Add the fish and coat in the polenta mixture. Brush a baking tray with some oil and arrange the coated fish on the tray. Grill the fish for 3–5 minutes until cooked through.

3. Divide the fish, rocket, avocado and pepper equally into four, putting the ingredients in one quarter of each tortilla. Drizzle over the yogurt dressing, then fold each tortilla into quarters to make a pocket. Serve immediately.

**GOES WELL WITH...**
*green salad*

# Prawn Gumbo

Preparation time 20 minutes • Cooking time about 45 minutes • Serves 4 • Per Serving 317 calories, 5g fat (of which 1g saturates), 43g carbohydrates, 25g protein, 5g fibre, 3.7g salt

1 tbsp vegetable oil

1 medium onion, finely sliced

2 celery sticks, finely chopped

2 green peppers, seeded and
   roughly chopped

1–2 red chillies, to taste, seeded
   and finely chopped

3 thyme sprigs

2 garlic cloves, crushed

2 × 400g cans chopped tomatoes

200g (7oz) okra, roughly chopped

1 litre (1¾ pint) vegetable stock

150g (5oz) basmati rice, rinsed

300g (11oz) cooked, peeled king
   prawns

salt and freshly ground black
   pepper

a large handful of fresh flat-leafed
   parsley, roughly chopped,
   to garnish

1. Heat the oil in a large pan. Add the onion, celery and peppers and gently fry for 5 minutes until beginning to soften. Stir in the chillies, thyme, garlic, tomatoes, okra and stock. Bring to the boil, then reduce the heat and simmer for 20 minutes.

2. Stir in the rice, reduce the heat and simmer for 20 minutes, stirring occasionally, until the rice is cooked and the liquid has been absorbed. Stir in the prawns, heat through and check the seasoning. Discard the thyme sprigs, garnish with the parsley and serve.

# Chilli Crab Noodles

Preparation time 10 minutes • Cooking time about 15 minutes • Serves 4 • Per Serving 334 calories, 8g fat
(of which 2g saturates), 51g carbohydrates, 18g protein, 2g fibre, 3.5g salt

**200g (7oz) medium egg noodles**
**1 tbsp vegetable oil**
**400g (14oz) frozen mixed
  vegetables**
**6 tbsp sweet chilli sauce**
**1 tbsp soy sauce**
**½ tbsp cornflour**
**100ml (3½fl oz) chicken or
  vegetable stock**
**170g canned crab, drained**
**a handful of coriander leaves,
  chopped**

1. Bring a pan of water to the boil and cook the noodles according to the pack instructions. Drain well and put to one side.

2. Heat the oil in a large wok until smoking. Add the mixed vegetables and stir-fry for 5 minutes or until piping hot.

3. In a small bowl, stir together the sweet chilli sauce, soy, cornflour and stock. Add the sauce to the wok and bubble for 1 minute, then toss through the noodles, crab and coriander. Check the seasoning and serve immediately.

**COOK'S TIP**
*If you don't have canned crab, any canned fish or fresh or frozen seafood would work just as well.*

# Creamy Prawn & Pea Penne

Preparation time 15 minutes • Cooking time about 15 minutes • Serves 4 • Per Serving 392 calories, 5g fat (of which 1g saturates), 64g carbohydrates, 30g protein, 9g fibre, 4g salt

**300g (11oz) wholewheat penne pasta**
**150g (5oz) frozen peas**
**½ tbsp oil**
**2 medium leeks, thinly sliced**
**1 garlic clove, crushed**
**300g (11oz) cooked peeled king prawns**
**zest and juice of 1 lemon**
**100g (3½oz) 2% fat Greek yogurt**
**salt and freshly ground black pepper**

**1.** Bring a large pan of salted water to the boil and cook the pasta according to the pack instructions, adding the peas for the final 2 minutes of cooking.

**2.** Meanwhile, heat the oil in a large frying pan and gently cook the leeks for 10 minutes, then add the garlic and prawns and cook for 2 minutes or until the prawns are heated through. Stir in the lemon zest and Greek yogurt.

**3.** When the pasta and peas are cooked to your liking, reserve one cupful of the cooking water, then drain. Stir the pasta and peas into the leek mixture. Add enough of the reserved pasta water to make a smooth sauce. Season well, adding lemon juice to taste. Serve immediately.

**HEALTHY TIP**
*Leeks are an excellent source of vitamin C, as well as iron and fibre.*

# Courgette & Goat's Cheese Spaghetti

Preparation time 10 minutes • Cooking time about 10 minutes • Serves 4 • Per Serving 393 calories, 9g fat (of which 4g saturates), 66g carbohydrates, 15g protein, 3g fibre, 0.3g salt

**350g (12oz) dried spaghetti**

**1 tbsp olive oil**

**1 garlic clove, finely chopped**

**½–1 red chilli, to taste, seeded and finely chopped**

**2 medium courgettes, coarsely grated**

**finely grated zest and juice of 1 lemon**

**75g (3oz) soft, crumbly goat's cheese**

**a small handful of fresh mint, finely shredded**

**salt and freshly ground black pepper**

1. Cook the spaghetti in a large pan of boiling water according to the pack instructions.

2. Meanwhile, heat the oil in a large frying pan, add the garlic and chilli and fry for 30 seconds, then add the courgettes and fry for a further 1 minute. Put to one side.

3. When the pasta is cooked to your liking, reserve a cupful of the cooking water before draining. Add the drained pasta to the courgette pan together with the lemon zest and juice. Crumble in most of the goat's cheese, then toss to combine, adding some of the reserved pasta water if the mixture seems dry.

4. Check the seasoning, then divide among four bowls. Sprinkle with the mint, the remaining goat's cheese and plenty of pepper. Serve immediately.

**HEALTHY TIP**

*Goat's cheese is lower in fat and has fewer calories than cow's milk cheese.*

# Blonde Pizza

Preparation time 20 minutes, plus rising • Cooking time 25 minutes • Serves 4 • Per Serving 365 calories, 9g fat (of which 5g saturates), 59g carbohydrates, 15g protein, 3g fibre, 0.3g salt

**300g (11oz) strong white bread flour, plus extra to dust**
**1 tsp fast-action dried yeast**
**1 tsp caster sugar**
**½ tsp extra virgin olive oil, plus extra to drizzle**
**1 small courgette, cut into ribbons with a peeler**
**½ red onion, finely sliced**
**125g (4oz) mozzarella ball, torn into pieces**
**1 red chilli, seeded and finely sliced**
**salt and freshly ground black pepper**
**a small handful of rocket to garnish**

**1.** Put the flour, yeast, sugar and ½ tsp salt into a large bowl. Quickly mix in 250ml (9fl oz) warm water to make a soft, but not sticky dough (add more flour/water as needed). Knead on a floured worksurface for 5 minutes. Form into a ball, cover with a teatowel and leave for 15 minutes.

**2.** Preheat the oven to 220°C (200°C fan oven) mark 7 and put a large non-stick baking sheet in to heat up. Roll out the dough to a thin circle about 38cm (15in) in diameter – keep dusting the surface with flour as needed. Carefully transfer the pizza base to the preheated baking sheet and brush the base with oil. Cook for 10 minutes.

**3.** Take the sheet out of the oven and scatter the courgette, red onion, mozzarella and chilli over the base. Put back into the oven for 15 minutes. Season and garnish with rocket, drizzle over the extra oil and serve immediately.

### FREEZE AHEAD

*Prepare to the end of step 1, but don't leave to rise. Transfer to an oiled freezer bag and freeze for up to a month. Defrost and complete the recipe to serve.*

# Mushroom & Two-grain Risotto

Preparation time 20 minutes • Cooking time about 25 minutes • Serves 4 • Per Serving 342 calories, 8g fat
(of which 4g saturates), 61g carbohydrates, 9g protein, 1g fibre, 2g salt

**200g (7oz) risotto rice, such as
  arborio or carnaroli**
**100g (3½oz) quinoa**
**1.1 litres (2 pints) vegetable stock**
**25g (1oz) butter**
**1 onion, finely chopped**
**250g pack chestnut mushrooms,
  sliced**
**4 fresh thyme sprigs, leaves picked**
**2 garlic cloves, crushed**
**a large handful of fresh rocket**
**salt and freshly ground black
  pepper**

1. Put the rice and quinoa into a large pan. Add the stock and bring to the boil. Reduce the heat to a gentle simmer, then cook, stirring frequently, until tender and thickened – about 20 minutes.

2. Meanwhile, heat the butter in a separate large frying pan and gently cook the onion for 10 minutes or until soft. Increase the heat to high and add the mushrooms. Cook, stirring frequently, for 5 minutes or until tender and any moisture has evaporated. Add the thyme leaves, garlic and some seasoning and cook for 1 minute more. Take off the heat and put to one side.

3. When the rice mixture is ready, stir the mushroom mixture and most of the rocket through it. Check the seasoning and divide among four bowls. Garnish with the remaining rocket and serve immediately.

# Saffron & Red Pepper Risotto

Preparation time 20 minutes • Cooking time about 20 minutes • Serves 4 • Per Serving 363 calories, 7g fat (of which 1g saturates), 69g carbohydrates, 5g protein, 1g fibre, 0.5g salt

1 tbsp extra virgin olive oil, plus extra to drizzle
300g (11oz) risotto rice
2 large pinches of saffron
150ml (¼ pint) white wine
200g (7oz) roasted red peppers, roughly chopped
50g (2oz) rocket
salt and freshly ground black pepper

1. Heat the oil in a large pan over a medium heat. Fry the rice and saffron for 1 minute, then add the white wine and leave to bubble until most of the liquid has been absorbed.

2. Measure 800ml (1¼ pint) of boiling water and add a ladleful to the rice pan and stir until the water has been fully absorbed. Continue this process until the rice is cooked, about 15–18 minutes.

3. Stir through the roasted red peppers and check the seasoning.

4. Serve immediately topped with rocket and a drizzle of extra virgin olive oil.

# Butter Bean Masala

Preparation time about 10 minutes • Cooking time about 10 minutes • Serves 1 • Per Serving 314 calories, 8g fat (of which 1g saturates), 44g carbohydrates, 19g protein, 21g fibre, 3.3g salt

½ tbsp vegetable oil

1 shallot, sliced

1 garlic clove, crushed

1 tsp garam masala

¼–½ red chilli, seeded and
  finely chopped

2 tomatoes, roughly chopped

410g can butter beans, drained
  and rinsed

a handful of fresh coriander or
  spinach, chopped

salt and freshly ground black
  pepper

**1.** Heat the oil in a pan, add the shallot and gently cook for 5 minutes. Stir in the garlic, garam masala and chilli and cook for 1 minute, then add the tomatoes and 100ml (3½fl oz) water. Simmer for 3 minutes, occasionally squashing the tomatoes with a wooden spoon.

**2.** Stir in the butter beans and heat through. Stir through the coriander or spinach and check the seasoning. Serve immediately.

# Lentil Chilli

Preparation time 15 minutes • Cooking time about 25 minutes • Serves 4 • Per Serving 307 calories, 5g fat (of which 1g saturates), 48g carbohydrates, 21g protein, 16g fibre, 1.7g salt

**1 tbsp vegetable oil**

**1 red onion, finely chopped**

**1 tsp each ground cumin, coriander and chilli powder**

**2 × 400g cans chopped tomatoes**

**1 vegetable stock cube, crumbled**

**2 × 400g cans lentils, drained and rinsed**

**400g can kidney beans, drained and rinsed**

**a handful of fresh coriander, chopped**

**boiled brown rice to serve**

**1.** Heat the oil in a large pan, add the onion and fry for 10 minutes until soft. Add the ground spices and cook for a further minute. Stir in the tomatoes, stock cube and lentils and simmer for 10 minutes until thickened.

**2.** Add the kidney beans and heat through. Stir through most of the coriander and check the seasoning. Garnish with the remaining coriander and serve.

**GOES WELL WITH...**
*brown rice or crisp flatbreads*

# Mushroom & Bean Hotpot

Preparation time 15 minutes • Cooking time 35 minutes • Serves 6 • Per Serving 280 calories, 10g fat (of which 1g saturates), 34g carbohydrates, 10g protein, 7g fibre, 1.3g salt

**3 tbsp olive oil**

**700g (1½lb) chestnut mushrooms, roughly chopped**

**1 large onion, finely chopped**

**2 tbsp plain flour**

**2 tbsp mild curry paste**

**150ml (¼ pint) dry white wine**

**400g can chopped tomatoes**

**2 tbsp sun-dried tomato paste**

**2 × 400g cans mixed beans, drained and rinsed**

**3 tbsp mango chutney**

**3 tbsp roughly chopped fresh coriander and mint**

1. Heat the oil in a large pan over a low heat. Add the chopped mushrooms and onion and fry until the onion is soft and dark golden. Stir in the flour and mild curry paste and cook for 1–2 minutes.

2. Add the wine, tomatoes, sun-dried tomato paste and beans and bring to the boil, then reduce the heat and simmer gently for 30 minutes or until most of the liquid has reduced. Stir in the mango chutney and chopped herbs before serving.

# Exotic Fruit Salad

Preparation time 10 minutes • Serves 4 • Per Serving 187 calories, 1g fat (of which 0g saturates), 47g carbohydrates, 2g protein, 6g fibre, 0.1g salt

**2 oranges**

**1 mango, peeled, stoned and chopped**

**450g (1lb) peeled and diced fresh pineapple**

**200g (7oz) blueberries**

**½ Charentais melon, cubed**

**grated zest and juice of 1 lime**

**1.** Using a sharp knife, peel the oranges, remove the pith and cut the flesh into segments. Put into a bowl.

**2.** Add the mango, pineapple, blueberries and melon to the bowl, then add the lime zest and juice. Gently mix together and serve immediately.

**HEALTHY TIP**

*This dessert is packed with vitamins C and betacarotene (see page 75). Fresh pineapple contains the enzyme bromelain, which aids digestion and is beneficial for inflammatory conditions such as sinusitis and rheumatoid arthritis.*

**TRY SOMETHING DIFFERENT**

*An easy way to get two brand new dishes is to:*

*• Use 2 peeled, seeded and chopped papayas instead of the pineapple.*

*• Mix the seeds of 2 passion fruit with the lime juice before adding to the salad.*

# Fruity Rice Pudding

Preparation time 10 minutes • Cooking time 1 hour, plus cooling and chilling • Serves 6 • Per Serving 323 calories, 17g fat (of which 10g saturates), 36g carbohydrates, 7g protein, 0.1g fibre, 0.2g salt

**125g (4oz) short-grain pudding rice**
**1.1 litres (2 pints) full-fat milk**
**1 tsp vanilla extract**
**3–4 tbsp caster sugar**
**200ml (7fl oz) whipping cream**
**6 tbsp wild lingonberry sauce**

**1.** Put the rice into a pan with 600ml (1 pint) cold water and bring to the boil, then reduce the heat and simmer until the liquid has evaporated. Add the milk and bring to the boil, then reduce the heat and simmer for 45 minutes or until the rice is very soft and creamy. Leave to cool.

**2.** Add the vanilla extract and sugar to the rice. Lightly whip the cream and fold through the pudding. Chill in the fridge for 1 hour.

**3.** Divide the rice mixture among six dishes and top with 1 tbsp lingonberry sauce.

### COOK'S TIP

*Although wild lingonberry sauce is used here, a spoonful of any fruit sauce or compote, such as strawberry or blueberry, will taste delicious.*

# Apple Galette

Preparation time 20 minutes • Cooking time about 35 minutes • Cuts into 8 pieces • Per Serving 344 calories, 16g fat (of which 10g saturates), 45g carbohydrates, 4g protein, 0.9g fibre, 0.5g salt

**plain flour to dust**
**500g pack puff pastry**
**8 tbsp apricot jam**
**4 Braeburn apples, cored**
   **and very thinly sliced**

**1.** Preheat the oven to 200°C (180°C fan oven) mark 6. Lightly dust a worksurface with flour and roll out the pastry until it measures roughly 25.5 × 35.5cm (10 × 14in) and is 5mm (¼in) thick. Trim the edges to neaten. Put on to a large baking tray and thoroughly prick the pastry all over with a fork, leaving a 1cm (½in) border unpricked around the edge.

**2.** Spread half the jam over the pricked pastry, then arrange apple slices on top, overlapping them to make neat rows.

**3.** Bake the tart for 30–35 minutes until the pastry is golden and the apples have just started to take on colour. When the tart is 5 minutes away from the end of the cooking time, heat the remaining jam with 2 tsp water until just boiling, then carefully brush all over the apples straight after you take the tart out of the oven. Serve in slices, warm or at room temperature.

**FREEZE AHEAD**
*Complete the recipe, then cool the finished glazed tart and cut into slices. Wrap each slice well in non-stick baking parchment and freeze for up to 1 month (wrapped slices can be stacked on top of each other). To serve, thaw at room temperature (about 1 hour) or arrange the frozen slices on a baking tray and warm through in a preheated 150°C (130°C fan oven) mark 2 oven for 15–20 minutes until thawed.*

# Banana Cake

Preparation time 20 minutes • Cooking time about 1 hour, plus cooling • Cuts into 10 slices
Per Serving 363 calories, 18g fat (of which 11g saturates), 50g carbohydrates, 3g protein, 1g fibre, 0.4g salt

125g (4oz) unsalted butter,
    softened, plus extra to grease
125g (4oz) light muscovado sugar
2 large eggs, lightly beaten
50g (2oz) smooth apple sauce
3 very ripe bananas, about 375g
    (13oz) peeled weight, mashed
1½ tsp mixed spice
150g (5oz) gluten-free plain flour
    blend
1 tsp gluten-free baking powder
a pinch of salt

**FOR THE ICING**
75g (3oz) unsalted butter, softened
100g (3½oz) icing sugar, sifted
50g (2oz) light muscovado sugar
½ tbsp milk (optional)

**1.** Preheat the oven to 180°C (160°C fan oven) mark 4. Grease the base and sides of a 900g (2lb) loaf tin and line with baking parchment.

**2.** Using a hand-held electric whisk, beat the butter and muscovado sugar in a large bowl until pale and creamy. Gradually whisk in the eggs, then the apple sauce. Stir in the bananas.

**3.** Sift the spice, flour, baking powder and salt into the bowl, then use a large metal spoon to fold in (the mixture may look a little curdled). Spoon the mixture into the prepared tin.

**4.** Bake for 50 minutes to 1 hour until risen and a skewer inserted into the centre comes out clean. Leave to cool in the tin for 10 minutes, then turn out on to a wire rack (leave the lining paper on) and leave to cool completely. When the cake is cold, remove the lining paper and put the cake on a serving plate.

**5.** To make the icing, whisk together the butter and both sugars until smooth. If needed, add a little milk to loosen. Spread over the top of the cooled cake. Serve in slices.

**GOES WELL WITH...**
*dried banana chips (for decoration)*

# Courgette Cake

Preparation time 30 minutes • Cooking time about 35 minutes, plus cooling • Cuts into 10 slices
Per Serving 359 calories, 17g fat (of which 2g saturates), 49g carbohydrates, 6g protein, 1g fibre, 0.5g salt

**150ml (¼ pint) vegetable oil, plus extra to grease**
**250g (9oz) self-raising flour, plus extra to dust**
**50g (2oz) pistachios (shelled weight)**
**3 medium eggs**
**175g (6oz) caster sugar**
**1 tsp vanilla extract**
**½ tsp bicarbonate of soda**
**2 small courgettes, about 225g (8oz), coarsely grated**

**FOR THE ICING**
**125g (4oz) icing sugar, sifted**
**1 tbsp roughly chopped pistachios**

**1.** Preheat the oven to 180°C (160°C fan oven) mark 4. Grease a 25.5cm (10in) kugelhopf or bundt tin. Lightly dust with flour and tap out the excess. Pulse the pistachios in a food processor until finely ground (or chop by hand), then put to one side.

**2.** Whisk the oil, eggs, sugar and vanilla extract together in a large bowl. Sift in the flour and bicarbonate of soda and stir to combine. Mix in the courgettes and pistachios. Tip into the prepared tin and level the surface.

**3.** Bake for 35 minutes or until golden and a skewer inserted into the centre comes out clean. Leave to cool in the tin for 5 minutes, then turn out on to a wire rack and leave to cool completely.

**4.** To make the icing, mix the icing sugar with enough water (1½–2 tbsp) to get a smooth, fairly thick icing. Slide the cake on to a cake stand or serving plate. Drizzle the icing over it, then scatter the chopped pistachios on top. Serve in slices.

**TRY SOMETHING DIFFERENT**
*This cake can also be made in a deep 20.5cm (8in) round cake tin. Follow the recipe, baking the cake for about 55 minutes.*

# UNDER 500 CALORIES

# Spanish Omelette

Preparation time 15 minutes • Cooking time about 45 minutes • Serves 4 • Per Serving 453 calories, 25g fat (of which 6g saturates), 38g carbohydrates, 22g protein, 3g fibre, 1.6g salt

**900g (2lb) potatoes, peeled and left whole**
**3–4 tbsp vegetable oil**
**1 onion, finely sliced**
**8 medium eggs**
**3 tbsp freshly chopped flat-leafed parsley**
**3 streaky bacon rashers**
**salt and freshly ground black pepper**

1. Add the potatoes to a pan of cold salted water, bring to the boil, reduce the heat and simmer for 15–20 minutes or until almost cooked. Drain and leave until cool enough to handle, then slice thickly.

2. Heat 1 tbsp oil in an 18cm (7in) non-stick frying pan (suitable for use under the grill). Add the onion and fry gently for 7–10 minutes until softened. Take the pan off the heat and put to one side.

3. Lightly beat the eggs in a bowl and season well.

4. Preheat the grill. Heat the remaining oil in the frying pan, then layer the potato slices, onion and 2 tbsp chopped parsley in the pan. Pour in the beaten eggs and cook for 5–10 minutes until the omelette is firm underneath. Meanwhile, grill the bacon until golden and crisp, and then break into pieces.

5. Put the omelette in the pan under the grill for 2–3 minutes until the top is just set. Scatter the bacon and remaining chopped parsley over the surface. Serve cut into wedges.

**GOES WELL WITH...**
*green salad*

# Eggs Benedict

Preparation time 15 minutes • Cooking time 10 minutes • Serves 4 • Per Serving 440 calories, 36g fat (of which 29g saturates), 17g carbohydrates, 14g protein, 0.7g fibre, 1.8g salt

**4 slices bread**
**4 medium eggs**
**150ml (¼ pint) hollandaise sauce**
**4 thin slices lean ham**
**fresh parsley sprigs to garnish**

**1.** Toast the bread on both sides. Poach the eggs. Gently warm the hollandaise sauce.

**2.** Top each slice of toast with a folded slice of ham, then with a poached egg. Finally, coat the eggs with hollandaise sauce.

**3.** Garnish each with a sprig of parsley and serve.

# Smoked Haddock Kedgeree

Preparation time 30 minutes, plus chilling (optional) • Cooking time about 15 minutes • Serves 4
Per Serving 429 calories, 20g fat (of which 11g saturates), 38g carbohydrates, 28g protein, 0.2g fibre, 3.1g salt

**175g (6oz) long-grain rice**
**450g (1lb) smoked haddock fillets**
**2 medium eggs, hard-boiled and**
   **shelled**
**75g (3oz) butter**
**salt and cayenne pepper**
**freshly chopped parsley to garnish**

1. Cook the rice in a pan of fast-boiling salted water until tender. Drain well and rinse under cold water.

2. Meanwhile, put the haddock in a large frying pan with just enough water to cover. Bring to simmering point, then simmer for 10–15 minutes until tender. Drain, skin and flake the fish, discarding the bones.

3. Chop one egg and slice the other into rings. Melt the butter in a pan, add the cooked rice, fish, chopped egg, salt and cayenne pepper, and stir over a medium heat for 5 minutes or until hot. Pile on to a warmed serving dish and garnish with parsley and the sliced egg.

# Mulligatawny Soup

Preparation time 25 minutes • Cooking time 40 minutes • Serves 4 • Per Serving 431 calories, 25g fat (of which 7g saturates), 20g carbohydrates, 32g protein, 2g fibre, 1.5g salt

3 rashers streaky bacon, rinded and finely chopped
550g (1¼lb) chicken portions
600ml (1 pint) hot chicken stock
1 carrot, sliced
1 celery stick, chopped
1 apple, cored and chopped
2 tsp curry powder
4 peppercorns, crushed
1 clove
1 bay leaf
1 tbsp plain flour
150ml (¼ pint) milk
50g (2oz) long-grain rice, cooked

1. Fry the bacon in a large pan until the fat begins to run. Do not allow the bacon to become brown.

2. Add the chicken and brown well. Drain the meat on kitchen paper and pour off the fat.

3. Put the bacon and chicken back into the pan and add the hot stock and the next seven ingredients. Cover the pan and simmer for about 30 minutes or until the chicken is tender.

4. Remove the chicken and leave to cool a little. Cut off the meat and put it back into the soup. Discard the clove and bay leaf and reheat the soup gently.

5. Mix the flour with a little cold water. Add to the soup with the milk and reheat without boiling.

6. Ladle the soup into four warmed bowls, spoon a mound of rice into each one and serve immediately.

**GOES WELL WITH...**
*crusty bread*

# Scotch Broth

Preparation time 15 minutes • Cooking time about 1 hour • Serves 4 • Per Serving 432 calories, 20g fat (of which 7g saturates), 46g carbohydrates, 20g protein, 5g fibre, 1.8g salt

**1 tbsp vegetable oil**

**250g (9oz) lamb neck fillets, cut into 2cm (¾in) cubes**

**2 parsnips, roughly chopped**

**2 carrots, roughly chopped**

**1 onion, finely chopped**

**1 potato, finely diced**

**3 smoked streaky bacon rashers, finely sliced**

**125g (4oz) pearl barley**

**1 litre (1¾ pints) lamb stock**

**75g (3oz) frozen peas**

**salt and freshly ground black pepper**

**a small handful of finely chopped fresh parsley to garnish**

**1.** Heat the oil over a high heat in a large casserole. Brown the lamb all over – do this in batches if necessary to stop the lamb from sweating rather than browning. Add the parsnips, carrots, onion, potato and bacon and fry for 3–5 minutes.

**2.** Add the pearl barley and mix well. Pour in the stock and stir well, scraping any sticky goodness from the bottom of the casserole. Bring to the boil, then reduce the heat, cover and simmer gently for 40–50 minutes until the lamb is tender.

**3.** Stir in the peas, heat through, then check the seasoning. Transfer to individual bowls, garnish the broth with parsley and serve.

# Chicken Caesar Salad

Preparation time about 20 minutes • Cooking time 12 minutes • Serves 4 • Per Serving 482 calories, 27g fat (of which 8g saturates), 8g carbohydrates, 61g protein, 2g fibre, 1.4g salt

2 tbsp olive oil

1 garlic clove, crushed

2 thick slices country-style bread, cubed

6 tbsp freshly grated Parmesan

1 cos lettuce, washed, chilled and cut into bite-size pieces

700g (1½lb) cooked chicken breast, sliced

**FOR THE DRESSING**

4 tbsp mayonnaise

2 tbsp lemon juice

1 tsp Dijon mustard

2 anchovy fillets, very finely chopped

salt and freshly ground black pepper

**1.** Preheat the oven to 180°C (160°C fan oven) mark 4. Put the oil, garlic and bread cubes into a bowl and toss well. Tip on to a baking sheet and bake in the oven for 10 minutes, turning halfway through.

**2.** Sprinkle the Parmesan over the croûtons and bake for 2 minutes or until the cheese has melted and the bread is golden.

**3.** Whisk all the dressing ingredients together in a small bowl with some seasoning.

**4.** Put the lettuce and sliced chicken into a bowl, pour the dressing over and toss to combine. Top with the cheese croûtons and serve.

# Warm Spiced Salad Niçoise

Preparation time 15 minutes • Cooking time 15 minutes • Serves 4 • Per Serving 480 calories, 28g fat (of which 6g saturates), 10g carbohydrates, 33g protein, 20g fibre, 0.6g salt

**350g (12oz) new potatoes, thickly sliced**
**175g (6oz) fine green beans**
**175g (6oz) cherry tomatoes, halved**
**1 small red onion, cut into thin wedges**
**4 × 150–175g (5–6oz) salmon fillets, skinned**
**15g (½oz) butter, melted**
**1 tbsp coriander seeds, crushed**
**½ tsp dried crushed chillies**
**4 tbsp Caesar Dressing (see page 156)**
**flaked sea salt and freshly ground black pepper**
**fresh chives to garnish**

1. Cook the potatoes in salted boiling water for 8–10 minutes until just tender, adding the beans for the final 2 minutes of cooking. Drain well, then transfer to a bowl and add the tomatoes and onion wedges.

2. Preheat the grill. Cut each salmon fillet into three strips. Place the strips in four piles on a baking sheet and brush each pile with the melted butter. Mix the crushed coriander seeds with the chillies and a little sea salt and sprinkle evenly over the salmon. Place under the hot grill and cook for 4–5 minutes until just cooked through.

3. Add 1 tbsp water to the Caesar Dressing to thin it slightly (it should be the consistency of single cream). Spoon three-quarters of the dressing over the vegetables and toss to coat. Season well.

4. Divide the vegetables among four serving plates, top with the salmon pieces and drizzle the remaining dressing around the edge of the salad. Garnish with chives and serve immediately.

# Quinoa & Halloumi Salad

Preparation time 15 minutes • Cooking time about 25 minutes • Serves 4 • Per Serving 435 calories, 25g fat (of which 11g saturates), 2g fibre, 33g carbohydrates, 22g protein, 0.8g salt

**200g (7oz) quinoa**
**150g (5oz) fresh or frozen peas**
**250g pack of halloumi**
**2 tbsp rapeseed oil, plus extra to brush**
**3 spring onions, finely sliced**
**70g bag rocket**
**finely grated zest and juice of 1 lemon**
**a small handful each of fresh mint and parsley, roughly chopped**
**salt and freshly ground black pepper**

**1.** Put the quinoa into a large pan and cover well with water. Bring to the boil, then reduce the heat and simmer until tender – about 20 minutes. Add the fresh or frozen peas to the pan for the final 2 minutes of cooking.

**2.** Meanwhile, preheat a griddle pan over a high heat. Cut the halloumi into 5mm (¼in) thick slices and brush both sides with oil. Grill for 4 minutes, turning once, or until the cheese has charred lines on both sides and has softened. Transfer to a board and leave to cool.

**3.** Put the spring onions and rocket into a large serving bowl. Put the oil, lemon zest and juice and plenty of seasoning into a small jug and mix well. Put to one side.

**4.** Drain the cooked quinoa mixture and run it under cold water to cool it quickly. Drain well and add to the serving bowl. Rip the halloumi into bite-size pieces and add to the bowl, together with the herbs and dressing. Toss everything together and check the seasoning before serving.

# Summer Couscous

Preparation time 10 minutes • Cooking time 20 minutes • Serves 4 • Per Serving 405 calories, 21g fat (of which 3g saturates), 49g carbohydrates, 21g protein, 5g fibre, 0.7g salt

**175g (6oz) baby plum tomatoes, halved**
**2 small aubergines, thickly sliced**
**2 large yellow peppers, seeded and roughly chopped**
**2 red onions, cut into thin wedges**
**2 fat garlic cloves, crushed**
**5 tbsp olive oil**
**250g (9oz) couscous**
**400g can chopped tomatoes**
**2 tbsp harissa paste**
**1 large bunch of fresh coriander, roughly chopped**
**salt and freshly ground black pepper**

1. Preheat the oven to 230°C (210°C fan oven) mark 8. Put the vegetables and garlic into a large roasting tin, drizzle 3 tbsp of the oil over them and season with salt and ground black pepper. Toss to coat. Roast for 20 minutes or until tender.

2. Meanwhile, put the couscous into a separate roasting tin, add 300ml (½ pint) cold water and leave to soak for 5 minutes. Stir in the chopped tomatoes and harissa and drizzle with the remaining oil. Pop in the oven next to the vegetables for 4–5 minutes to warm through.

3. Stir the coriander into the couscous and season. Add the vegetables, stir through and serve.

# Chicken Chow Mein

Preparation time 15 minutes • Cooking time about 12 minutes • Serves 4 • Per Serving 436 calories, 11g fat
(of which 3g saturates), 49g carbohydrates, 38g protein, 3g fibre, 1.3g salt

**200g (7oz) medium egg noodles**
**1 tsp sesame oil**
**400g (14oz) skinless chicken**
   **breasts, cut into finger-size**
   **strips**
**1½ tsp Chinese five-spice powder**
**1 tbsp vegetable oil**
**2 red peppers, seeded and sliced**
**5 spring onions, thinly sliced**
**a large handful of bean sprouts**
**salt and freshly ground black**
   **pepper**

**FOR THE SAUCE**
**2.5cm (1in) piece fresh root ginger,**
   **peeled and grated**
**2 garlic cloves, crushed**
**1 tbsp cornflour**
**1½ tbsp oyster sauce**
**1½ tbsp tomato ketchup**
**2 tbsp light soy sauce**

**1.** Start by making the sauce. In a small bowl, mix together the ginger, garlic and cornflour. Whisk in the remaining sauce ingredients and put to one side.

**2.** Bring a medium pan of water to the boil and cook the noodles according to the pack instructions. Drain well, then toss through the sesame oil to stop them sticking together and put to one side.

**3.** Put the chicken strips into a large bowl. Toss through the five-spice powder and some seasoning.

**4.** Heat the vegetable oil in a large wok until smoking. Add the chicken and stir-fry for 5 minutes until golden and cooked through – if you find the chicken is sticking, add a splash of water. Add the peppers, spring onions and bean sprouts and cook for 1–2 minutes until just wilted. Add the noodles and sauce and heat through. Check the seasoning and serve.

# Paella

Preparation time 15 minutes • Cooking time about 30 minutes • Serves 4 • Per Serving 425 calories, 6g fat
(of which 1g saturates), 67g carbohydrates, 21g protein, 2g fibre, 0.9g salt

1 tbsp vegetable oil

1 large onion, thinly sliced

4 boneless, skinless chicken
    thighs, roughly chopped

2 garlic cloves, finely chopped

a pinch of saffron

¼ tsp smoked paprika

1 red pepper, seeded and finely
    diced

300g (11oz) paella rice

1.1 litres (2 pints) hot chicken stock

180g tub mussel meat, drained if in
    brine

a large handful of fresh curly
    parsley, roughly chopped

salt and freshly ground black
    pepper

1. Gently heat the oil in a large paella pan or frying pan. Add the onion and cook for 5 minutes. Add the chicken and cook for 3 minutes. Stir in the garlic, saffron and paprika and cook for 1 minute to release the flavours.

2. Stir in the red pepper and rice. Pour in the hot stock and leave to simmer gently for 20 minutes, stirring occasionally, or until the rice is cooked through.

3. Stir in the mussels and parsley and check the seasoning. Serve immediately.

# Turkey Meatballs with Barbecue Sauce

Preparation time 15 minutes • Cooking time about 20 minutes • Serves 4 • Per Serving 467 calories, 11g fat (of which 3g saturates), 51g carbohydrates, 41g protein, 2g fibre, 2.1g salt

**500g (1lb 2oz) turkey mince**
**2 tsp ground coriander**
**½–1 red chilli, seeded and finely chopped**
**½ tbsp olive oil**
**1 onion, finely chopped**
**1 garlic clove, crushed**
**400g can chopped tomatoes**
**2 tbsp soy sauce**
**3 tbsp tomato ketchup**
**salt and freshly ground black pepper**
**a little chopped fresh coriander, chives or parsley to garnish**
**200g white rice, boiled**

**1.** Preheat the oven to 200°C (180°C fan oven) mark 6 and line a baking tray with baking parchment.

**2.** Put the turkey mince into a large bowl, add the ground coriander, chilli and plenty of seasoning and mix through (using your hands is easiest). Form into walnut-sized meatballs – you should have about 20.

**3.** Arrange the meatballs on the prepared tray and cook in the oven, turning midway, for 20 minutes or until golden and cooked through.

**4.** Meanwhile, heat the oil in a large pan over a medium heat. Add the onion and fry for 10 minutes or until softened. Stir in the garlic and cook for 1 minute, then add the tomatoes, soy sauce, ketchup and seasoning. Bring to the boil, then reduce the heat and simmer for 10 minutes or until thickened slightly.

**5.** Add the meatballs to the sauce and stir gently to coat. Garnish with fresh herbs and serve with boiled white rice.

**TRY SOMETHING DIFFERENT**
*For a healthier alternative, serve with wholegrain rice.*

# Spiced Lamb Kebabs with Crunchy Coleslaw

Preparation time 10 minutes • Cooking time about 15 minutes • Serves 4 • Per Serving 400 calories, 15g fat (of which 6g saturates), 39g carbohydrates, 27g protein, 4g fibre, 0.9g salt

**1 red onion**

**1 garlic clove, roughly chopped**

**1 tsp each ground cumin, coriander and cayenne pepper**

**350g (12oz) lean lamb mince**

**a small handful of fresh mint, roughly chopped**

**½ small red cabbage, finely shredded**

**150g (5oz) low-fat natural yogurt**

**juice of ½ lemon**

**1 tbsp tahini**

**4 pitta breads**

**2 large tomatoes, sliced**

**salt and freshly ground black pepper**

**1.** Preheat the grill to medium. Chop half the onion and put into a food processor with the garlic, spices, lamb mince and most of the mint. Season well and whiz until combined. Divide the mixture into eight and form each piece into a patty. Transfer the patties to a non-stick baking tray and grill for 10–12 minutes, turning once, until cooked through.

**2.** Finely slice the remaining onion and put into a large bowl with the shredded cabbage. In a small bowl, whisk together the yogurt, lemon juice, tahini and remaining mint. Stir half the yogurt dressing through the cabbage mixture and check the seasoning.

**3.** Toast the pittas and cut horizontally through the middle to make pockets. Bring the pittas, patties, tomatoes, coleslaw and remaining dressing to the table and let people tuck in.

**GOES WELL WITH…**
*lemon wedges to squeeze over the kebab filling*

# Moroccan Lamb Burgers

Preparation time 20 minutes • Cooking time about 20 minutes • Serves 4 • Per Serving 447 calories, 22g fat
(of which 10g saturates), 29g carbohydrates, 34g protein, 2g fibre, 0.6g salt

1 tsp ground cumin
½ tbsp coriander seeds
1 fat garlic clove
600g (1lb 5oz) lamb mince
finely grated zest of ½ orange
50g (2oz) ready to eat dried
　apricots, finely chopped
½ tbsp vegetable oil
100g (3½oz) natural yogurt
½–1 tsp harissa paste, to taste
2 tbsp freshly chopped mint
a large handful of watercress
4 flour tortillas or white khobez
　wraps
salt and freshly ground black
　pepper

1. In a pestle and mortar, pound the cumin, coriander, garlic and plenty of seasoning until fairly smooth. Scrape into a large bowl and stir in the lamb mince, orange zest and apricots. Divide the and shape each portion into a flattened patty.

2. Heat the oil in a frying pan over a medium heat and cook for 15–18 minutes, turning occasionally, until cooked through.

3. Meanwhile, in a small bowl, stir together the yogurt, harissa, mint and some seasoning. Serve the burgers and watercress wrapped in the tortillas or wraps, drizzled with the harissa sauce.

# Irish Stew

Preparation time 15 minutes • Cooking time about 2¼ hours • Serves 4 • Per Serving 419 calories, 20g fat (of which 9g saturates), 24g carbohydrates, 46g protein, 3g fibre, 0.6g salt

**700g (1½lb) middle neck lamb cutlets, fat trimmed**
**2 onions, thinly sliced**
**450g (1lb) potatoes, thinly sliced**
**1 tbsp freshly chopped flat-leafed parsley, plus extra to garnish**
**1 tbsp dried thyme**
**300ml (½ pint) hot lamb stock**
**salt and freshly ground black pepper**

1. Preheat the oven to 170°C (150°C fan oven) mark 3. Layer the meat, onions and potatoes in a deep casserole dish, sprinkling some herbs and salt and ground black pepper between each layer. Finish with a layer of potato, overlapping the slices neatly.

2. Pour the hot stock over the potatoes, then cover with greaseproof paper and a lid. Cook in the oven for about 2 hours until the meat is tender.

3. Preheat the grill. Take the lid off the casserole and remove the paper. Put under the grill and brown the top of the potatoes. Sprinkle with chopped parsley and serve immediately.

# Easy Peasy Pork Chops

Preparation time 10 minutes • Cooking time 40 minutes • Serves 4 • Per Serving 497 calories, 33g fat (of which 13g saturates), 21g carbohydrates, 28g protein, 3g fibre, 0.4g salt

**4 pork loin chops**
**½ tbsp sunflower oil**
**400g (14oz) new potatoes, halved lengthways**
**2 apples, cored and cut into 8 wedges**
**75ml (3fl oz) each cider and hot vegetable stock**
**50g (2oz) blue Wensleydale cheese**
**salt and freshly ground black pepper**
**1 tbsp roughly chopped sage leaves, to garnish**

**1.** Preheat the oven to 230°C (210°C fan oven) mark 8. Snip the fat on the pork chops at 2cm (¾in) intervals with a pair of scissors – this will stop the chops curling as they cook. Heat the oil in a flameproof roasting tin set over a medium heat on the hob, then brown the chops on both sides and put to one side.

**2.** Put the potatoes in the same roasting tin and coat in the oil. Roast for 15 minutes.

**3.** Nestle the chops and apples among the potatoes, then pour in the cider and hot stock. Season. Put back into the oven for 15 minutes or until the pork is cooked through.

**4.** Crumble over the cheese and put back into the oven for 2–3 minutes until melted. Garnish with sage and spoon over the cooking juices to serve.

# Sticky Ribs with Rice & Beans

Preparation time 15 minutes • Cooking time about 55 minutes • Serves 4 • Per Serving 448 calories, 7g fat (of which 3g saturates), 82g carbohydrates, 20g protein, 6g fibre, 3g salt

**125g (4oz) tomato ketchup**
**1½ tbsp soy sauce**
**1½ tbsp white wine vinegar**
**3 tbsp runny honey**
**1½ tsp mixed spice**
**½ tsp hot chilli powder**
**1.5kg (3¼lb) individual pork spare ribs**
**250g (9oz) basmati rice**
**400g can kidney beans, drained and rinsed**
**a large handful of fresh coriander, chopped**

**1.** Preheat the oven to 200°C (180°C fan oven) mark 6. Line a large roasting tin with a double layer of foil. In a large bowl, mix together the first six ingredients. Add the ribs to the bowl and stir to coat completely, then empty the ribs and glaze into the lined roasting tin and spread out evenly.

**2.** Cover with foil and cook in the oven for 20 minutes. Uncover, then turn the ribs and put back into the oven for 30–35 minutes, turning in the glaze occasionally, until they're dark and sticky (most of the liquid should have evaporated).

**3.** Meanwhile, cook the rice according to the pack instructions, adding the kidney beans for the final 2 minutes of cooking. Drain well and stir in the coriander. Serve the rice with the ribs.

**GOES WELL WITH…**
green salad

**GET AHEAD**
The ribs can be marinated and stored in the fridge up to a day before. Use a non-reactive container such as a glass bowl or plastic food storage box.

# Beef Fajitas

Preparation time 10 minutes • Cooking time about 10 minutes • Serves 4 • Per Serving 442 calories, 15g fat (of which 5g saturates), 41g carbohydrates, 38g protein, 4g fibre, 0.7g salt

**1 tbsp olive oil**

**600g (1lb 5oz) rump or fillet steak, thinly sliced**

**3 peppers, seeded and finely sliced**

**1 tbsp Cajun spice**

**4 flour tortillas**

**4 tbsp guacamole or soured cream**

**1.** Heat the oil in a large frying pan and cook the rump or fillet steak over a medium-high heat for 2–3 minutes for medium-rare meat or longer, if you like.

**2.** Transfer the steak to a bowl, cover with foil and leave to rest.

**3.** Add the peppers to the pan with a splash of water and cook for 2–3 minutes until beginning to soften.

**4.** Put the beef back into the pan, stir in the Cajun spice and heat through. Check the seasoning.

**5.** Serve the beef mixture in 4 flour tortillas, each topped with 1 tbsp guacamole or soured cream.

# Beef & Dumpling Stew

Preparation time 25 minutes • Cooking time 3 hours 40 minutes • Serves 6 • Per Serving 403 calories, 17g fat (of which 7g saturates), 40g carbohydrates, 22g protein, 5g fibre, 1.5g salt

2 tbsp sunflower oil

450g (1lb) stewing steak, cut into 5cm (2in) pieces

2 medium onions, finely sliced

2 carrots, sliced

350g (12oz) swede, peeled and cut into chunks

2 tbsp plain flour

150ml (¼ pint) Irish dry stout

300ml (½ pint) hot beef stock

2 tsp dark brown sugar

1 tbsp Worcestershire sauce

1 bay leaf

1 fresh thyme sprig

## FOR THE DUMPLINGS

200g (7oz) plain flour

3 tsp baking powder

½ tsp dry English mustard

½ tsp salt

50g (2oz) low-fat vegetable suet

2 tbsp mixed freshly chopped herbs (we used parsley, sage, rosemary, and thyme)

1. Preheat the oven to 150°C (130°C fan oven) mark 2. Heat 1 tbsp oil in a flameproof casserole dish and brown the beef in batches. Put to one side.

2. Add the remaining oil to the pan and gently fry the onions and carrots for 10 minutes until softened. Add the swede and cook for 2 minutes.

3. Put the beef back into the pan, sprinkle in the flour and cook for 1 minute. Gradually stir in the stout and hot stock. Add the sugar, Worcestershire sauce, bay leaf and thyme, then bring to the boil. Cover and cook in the oven for 3 hours.

4. To make the dumplings, sift the flour, baking powder, mustard and salt into a bowl. Stir in the suet and mixed herbs. Using a flat-bladed knife, stir in about 150ml (¼ pint) cold water to make a soft but not too sticky dough.

5. Divide the dough into 12 and roll into balls. Drop on to the stew, spaced evenly apart. Cover and cook for 20 minutes until puffed up. Remove the lid and put back into the oven for 5 minutes to finish cooking the dumplings, then serve.

# Penne Puttanesca

Preparation time 15 minutes • Cooking time about 25 minutes • Serves 4 • Per Serving 427 calories, 9g fat (of which 2g saturates), 72g carbohydrates, 18g protein, 4g fibre, 1.6g salt

**350g (12oz) dried penne pasta**
**1 tbsp olive oil**
**1 onion, finely chopped**
**400g can chopped tomatoes**
**2 tsp dried oregano**
**120g can boneless, skinless**
**    sardine fillets, drained**
**50g (2oz) black olives, pitted**
**salt and freshly ground black**
**    pepper**
**a small handful of fresh curly**
**    parsley, chopped, to garnish**

**1.** Bring a large pan of salted water to the boil and cook the pasta according to the pack instructions. Strain well, keeping a cupful of the cooking water to one side.

**2.** Meanwhile, heat the oil in a large pan and fry the onion for 10 minutes or until softened but not coloured. Add the tomatoes and oregano, then bring the mixture to the boil, reduce the heat and simmer for 15 minutes until thickened. Stir in the sardines and olives – the stirring should help break up the fish slightly.

**3.** Add the pasta to the sauce and toss well to combine. Add a little of the reserved pasta water if the mixture looks too dry. Check the seasoning, then divide among four bowls and garnish with parsley. Serve immediately.

# Pasta with Goat's Cheese & Sunblush Tomatoes

Preparation time 5 minutes • Cooking time 10 minutes • Serves 4 • Per Serving 409 calories, 12g fat (of which 4g saturates), 64g carbohydrates, 14g protein, 3g fibre, 0.4g salt

**300g (11oz) conchiglie pasta**
**2 tbsp olive oil**
**1 red pepper, seeded and chopped**
**1 yellow pepper, seeded and chopped**
**½ tbsp sun-dried tomato paste**
**75g (3oz) sunblush tomatoes**
**75g (3oz) soft goat's cheese**
**2 tbsp freshly chopped parsley**
**salt and freshly ground black pepper**

**1.** Cook the pasta in a large pan of lightly salted boiling water according to the pack instructions until al dente.

**2.** Meanwhile, heat the oil in a pan and fry the red and yellow peppers for 5–7 minutes until softened and just beginning to brown. Add the tomato paste and cook for a further minute. Add a ladleful of pasta cooking water to the pan and simmer for 1–2 minutes to make a sauce.

**3.** Drain the pasta and put back into the pan. Pour the sauce on top, then add the tomatoes, goat's cheese and parsley. Toss together until the cheese begins to melt, then season with ground black pepper and serve.

# Wrapped Monkfish with Milanese Risotto

Preparation time 25 minutes • Cooking time about 30 minutes • Serves 6 • Per Serving 499 calories, 13g fat (of which 6g saturates), 50g carbohydrates, 44g protein, 3g fibre, 1.3g salt

**6 × 175g (6oz) monkfish fillets, skinless**
**6 Parma ham slices**
**25g (1oz) butter**
**salt and freshly ground black pepper**

**FOR THE RISOTTO**
**1 tbsp extra virgin olive oil, plus extra to drizzle**
**1 onion, finely chopped**
**2 large pinches of saffron**
**300g (11oz) risotto rice**
**125ml (4fl oz) dry white wine**
**1.4 litre (2½ pints) fish or vegetable stock**
**200g (7oz) fine asparagus, cut into 2.5cm (1in) pieces**
**200g (7oz) peas, fresh or frozen**
**1 large courgette, cut into 1cm (½in) pieces**
**75g (3oz) Parmesan, grated, plus shavings to serve**
**large handful pea shoots**

**1.** Start by making the risotto. Heat the oil in a large pan and fry the onion for 10 minutes until softened. Meanwhile, wrap each fish fillet in a slice of Parma ham, season and put to one side.

**2.** Stir the saffron and rice into onion pan. Cook, stirring, for 1 minute, then add the wine and leave to bubble for a few minutes. Add a quarter of the stock and cook, stirring occasionally, until most of it has been absorbed. Continue adding big glugs of stock, stirring occasionally, until the rice is nearly tender, about 18 minutes (you may not need all the stock).

**3.** A few minutes before the rice is ready, add the asparagus, peas and courgette. When the rice is cooked and the veg are tender, take off the heat and stir in the Parmesan. Check the seasoning.

**4.** Ten minutes before the rice is due to be ready, heat the butter in a large frying pan over a medium heat until foaming. Cook the monkfish parcels for 10 minutes, turning once, until cooked through.

**GET AHEAD**
*Prepare to the end of step 2 up to a day ahead. Spread the risotto on a tray. When cool, cover and chill. Cover and chill the wrapped fish. To serve, put the risotto into a pan, add some stock and reheat (stirring).*

# Squash Risotto with Hazelnut Butter

Preparation time 20 minutes • Cooking time about 50 minutes • Serves 4 • Per Serving 474 calories, 15g fat
(of which 4g saturates), 79g carbohydrates, 8g protein, 4g fibre, 1.3g salt

1 tbsp vegetable oil

500g (1lb 2oz) butternut squash, peeled and cut into 2cm (¾in) cubes

1 onion, finely chopped

1 garlic clove, finely chopped

300g (11oz) risotto rice, such as Arborio or carnaroli

50ml (2fl oz) white wine

1.1 litres (2 pints) hot vegetable stock

25g (1oz) butter

40g (1½oz) blanched hazelnuts, chopped

4 fresh sage leaves, finely sliced

salt and freshly ground black pepper

**1.** Heat half the oil in a large pan over a medium heat. Fry the squash, tossing occasionally, for 15–20 minutes until tender. Lift the squash out of the pan and put on a plate.

**2.** Add the remaining oil to the pan and gently fry the onion for 10 minutes or until tender. Stir in the garlic and rice and cook for 2 minutes or until the rice turns translucent. Stir in the wine and let the mixture bubble, stirring frequently, until the liquid has evaporated.

**3.** Gradually add the hot stock, one ladleful at a time, adding another ladleful only when the previous one has been absorbed. Stir well after each addition. Continue until the rice is nearly cooked – this will take about 15 minutes.

**4.** Gently stir the cooked squash into the risotto and reheat. Check the seasoning, then cover the pan with a lid and put to one side.

**5.** Heat the butter and hazelnuts together in a small frying pan until the butter is light brown and the nuts are lightly toasted, then add the sage. Divide the risotto among four warmed bowls, garnish with the hazelnut butter and serve.

# Crispy-crumbed Cabbage Linguine

Preparation time 15 minutes • Cooking time about 15 minutes • Serves 4 • Per Serving 475 calories, 9g fat (of which 1g saturates), 87g carbohydrates, 17g protein, 6g fibre, 1.6g salt

**400g (14oz) dried linguine or spaghetti**

**2 tbsp extra virgin olive oil**

**50g (2oz) fresh white breadcrumbs**

**300g (11oz) Savoy cabbage, shredded**

**2 garlic cloves, crushed**

**50g can anchovies in olive oil**

**finely grated zest of 1 lemon**

**a small handful of fresh parsley, roughly chopped**

**salt and freshly ground black pepper**

**1.** Bring a large pan of salted water to the boil and cook the pasta according to the pack instructions.

**2.** Meanwhile, heat 1 tbsp of the oil in a large, deep frying pan. Cook the breadcrumbs, stirring frequently, until golden and crisp – about 5 minutes. Tip on to a plate and put to one side.

**3.** Put the frying pan back on to the heat and add the remaining oil. Stir in the cabbage and garlic and fry for 1 minute, then add two ladlefuls of pasta cooking water and cook until the cabbage is just tender. Add the anchovies with their oil and some ground black pepper, stirring to break up the fish. Put to one side.

**4.** Drain the pasta well and put back into the empty pan. Add the lemon zest and the cabbage mixture and toss through, then check the seasoning. Divide the linguine among four bowls and sprinkle the fried crumbs and the parsley over. Serve immediately.

# Easy Veggie Pad Thai

Preparation time 15 minutes • Cooking time 10 minutes • Serves 2 • Per Serving 440 calories, 25g fat (of which 5g saturates), 36g carbohydrates, 19g protein, 6g fibre, 0.3g salt

2 tbsp groundnut oil

2 medium eggs, beaten

2 spring onions, cut into chunks

¼ red chilli, chopped

1 red pepper, seeded and finely sliced

1 carrot, finely sliced

1 garlic clove, crushed

juice of ½ lime

1 tbsp tamarind paste

125g (4oz) bean sprouts

200g (7oz) straight-to-wok ribbon noodles

a handful each of freshly chopped coriander and mint

2 tbsp roasted peanuts, chopped

salt and freshly ground black pepper

**1.** Heat 1 tbsp oil in a wok or non-stick pan. Add the eggs, then stir-fry until just set. Season with salt and ground black pepper, then scoop out and put to one side.

**2.** Heat the remaining 1 tbsp oil in the wok and add the spring onions, chilli, red pepper, carrot and garlic. Stir-fry for 3–5 minutes, adding a splash of water if you need to.

**3.** Stir in the lime juice and tamarind, then add the bean sprouts, cooked egg and noodles. Mix well and heat through. Sprinkle with the herbs and peanuts and serve.

# Griddled Polenta Ratatouille Stack

Preparation time 30 minutes • Cooking time about 55 minutes plus cooling • Serves 4 • Per Serving 427 calories, 18g fat (of which 6g saturates), 46g carbohydrates, 21g protein, 6g fibre, 0.7g salt

**1 tbsp olive oil, plus extra to grease and drizzle**
**1 red onion, finely chopped**
**2 courgettes (total weight about 400g/14oz), finely diced**
**1 aubergine, finely diced**
**1 green pepper, seeded and finely diced**
**1 large garlic clove, finely chopped**
**2 × 400g cans chopped tomatoes**
**a large pinch of sugar**
**750ml (1¼ pints) strong vegetable stock**
**175g (6oz) instant dry polenta**
**75g (3oz) mature Cheddar, finely grated**
**4 medium eggs**
**a large handful of fresh basil leaves, torn**
**salt and freshly ground black pepper**

**1.** Heat the oil in a large pan and fry the onion gently for 10 minutes or until soft. Turn up the heat to medium and add the courgettes, aubergine and green pepper, then fry for 8–10 minutes until lightly coloured. Stir in the garlic, tomatoes and sugar and simmer for 10–15 minutes until thick and pulpy.

**2.** Meanwhile, line a rough 22 × 30.5cm (8½ × 12in) baking tray with baking parchment. Pour the stock into a large pan and bring to the boil, then stir in the polenta. Reduce the heat and simmer hard for 5 minutes, stirring continuously (take care – it may bubble volcanically), until the mixture thickens. Stir in the cheese and lots of seasoning, then tip the mixture on to the prepared tray and spread to the edges to make an even 1cm (½in) thick layer. Leave to cool for 10 minutes or until set.

**3.** Cut the polenta into 12 equal squares. Grease a griddle pan really well, then heat over a high heat until it is smoking hot. Add a few of the polenta squares and fry for 4 minutes until griddle lines appear, then flip over and cook for a further 4 minutes on the other side. Grease the pan well between batches, and cook the remainder of the polenta squares in the same way.

**4.** Meanwhile, bring a medium pan of water to the boil. Crack an egg into a cup or ramekin. Swirl the water to create a 'whirlpool', then carefully tip in the egg. Crack another egg into the cup and add to the water. Reduce the heat and simmer for 3–4 minutes until the whites are set and the yolks soft – lift an egg out with a slotted spoon and gently prod with your finger to check. Transfer the cooked eggs to a shallow dish of warm water. Repeat with the remaining eggs.

**5.** Stir the basil into the ratatouille and season to taste. To assemble each serving, layer up three polenta squares with ratatouille between them, then top with a poached egg. Drizzle a little olive oil over, sprinkle with plenty of ground black pepper and serve.

**GOES WELL WITH…**
green salad

# Goat's Cheese & Onion Slice

Preparation time 10 minutes • Cooking time 30 minutes • Serves 4 • Per Serving 466 calories, 31g fat
(of which 13g saturates), 41g carbohydrates, 10g protein, 1g fibre, 1.1g salt

**375g pack ready-rolled puff pastry**

**4 tbsp caramelised red onion relish
  or red onion marmalade**

**125g (4oz) marinated artichoke
  pieces**

**125g (4oz) cherry tomatoes, halved**

**100g (3½oz) button mushrooms,
  halved**

**50g (2oz) goat's cheese**

**1 tbsp extra virgin olive oil**

**salt and freshly ground black
  pepper**

**a large handful of rocket to garnish**

1. Preheat the oven to 200°C (180°C fan oven) mark 6. Unroll the pastry and lay on a baking tray. Use a knife to score a border 2cm (¾in) from the edges – but don't cut through. Prick the inside border with a fork and cook for 8–10 minutes until the pastry starts to puff.

2. Take out of the oven and press down the pastry inside the border. Spread the relish or marmalade inside the border. Scatter over the artichokes, tomatoes and mushrooms. Crumble over the goat's cheese and drizzle over the oil. Season with salt and ground black pepper.

3. Put back into the oven for 15–20 minutes until the pastry has risen and is golden. Garnish with rocket and serve.

# Bread & Butter Pudding

Preparation time 10 minutes, plus soaking • Cooking time 40 minutes • Serves 4 • Per Serving 450 calories, 13g fat (of which 5g saturates), 70g carbohydrates, 16g protein, 1g fibre, 1.1g salt

**50g (2oz) butter, softened, plus extra to grease**
**275g (10oz) white farmhouse bread, cut into 1cm (½in) slices, crusts removed**
**50g (2oz) raisins or sultanas**
**3 medium eggs**
**450ml (¾ pint) milk**
**3 tbsp golden icing sugar, plus extra to dust**

**1.** Lightly grease four 300ml (½ pint) gratin dishes or one 1.1 litre (2 pint) ovenproof dish. Butter the bread, then cut into quarters to make triangles. Arrange the bread in the dish(es) and sprinkle with the raisins or sultanas.

**2.** Beat the eggs, milk and sugar in a bowl. Pour the mixture over the bread and leave to soak for 10 minutes. Preheat the oven to 180°C (160°C fan oven) mark 4.

**3.** Bake the pudding(s) in the oven for 30–40 minutes. Dust with icing sugar to serve.

# Raspberry & Peach Cake

Preparation time 15 minutes • Cooking time about 1½ hours, plus cooling • Cuts into 8 slices • Per Serving
405 calories, 24g fat (of which 14g saturates), 44g carbohydrates, 7g protein, 2g fibre, 0.8g salt

**200g (7oz) unsalted butter, melted**
  **plus extra to grease**
**250g (9oz) self-raising flour, sifted**
**175g (6oz) light muscovado sugar**
**4 medium eggs, beaten**
**125g (4oz) raspberries**
**3 large almost-ripe peaches or**
  **nectarines, halved, stoned**
  **and diced**
**4 tbsp apricot jam**
**juice of ½ lemon**

1. Preheat the oven to 190°C (170°C fan oven) mark 5. Grease a 20.5cm (8in) springform cake tin and base-line with baking parchment.

2. Put the flour and sugar into a large bowl and make a well in the centre. Add the melted butter and the eggs and mix well.

3. Spread half the mixture over the bottom of the prepared tin and add half the raspberries and sliced peaches or nectarines. Spoon the remaining cake mixture over the top and smooth over, then add the remaining raspberries and peaches or nectarines, pressing them down into the mixture slightly.

4. Bake for 1–1¼ hours until risen and golden and a skewer inserted into the centre comes out clean. Remove from the oven and leave to cool in the tin for 10 minutes. Turn out of the tin, peel off the lining paper and place the cake on a serving plate.

5. Warm the jam and lemon juice together in a small pan and brush over the cake to glaze. Serve warm or at room temperature.

| | |
|---|---|
| BEANS, LENTILS, NUTS & SEEDS | 202 |
| BEVERAGES | 203 |
| BISCUITS (SAVOURY) & CEREAL BARS | 205 |
| BISCUITS (SWEET) & BARS | 206 |
| BREAD & BAKERY | 207 |
| BREAKFAST CEREALS | 208 |
| CAKES, PASTRIES & BUNS | 209 |
| CHEESE, CREAM, MILK & YOGURT | 210 |
| CONFECTIONERY & ICE CREAM | 212 |
| CRISPS & SNACKS | 214 |
| EATING OUT & TAKEAWAYS | 216 |
| EGGS | 218 |
| FATS, OILS & SPREADS | 219 |
| FISH & SEAFOOD | 220 |
| FISH PRODUCTS | 221 |
| FRUIT | 222 |
| MEAT | 224 |
| PASTA & PASTA DISHES | 227 |
| PASTRY & SAVOURY PIES | 228 |
| PIZZA | 228 |
| PUDDINGS | 229 |
| RICE, NOODLES & RICE DISHES | 230 |
| SALADS | 231 |
| SAUCES & DRESSINGS | 232 |
| SOUPS | 233 |
| STORECUPBOARD INGREDIENTS | 234 |
| VEGETABLES | 234 |
| VEGETARIAN PRODUCTS | 236 |

# A–Z CALORIE
# COUNTS

| Beans, lentils, nuts & seeds | Av Portion | Calories | Fat, g | Saturated fat, g | Carbohydrate, g | Protein, g | Fibre, g |
|---|---|---|---|---|---|---|---|
| **BEANS & LENTILS** | | | | | | | |
| Baked beans | 200g (1 small can) | 162 | 1.0 | 0.2 | 30 | 9.6 | 7.0 |
| Baked beans, reduced sugar | 200g (1 small can) | 148 | 1.0 | 0.2 | 26 | 11 | 7.6 |
| Black-eye beans, dried, boiled | 120g (4 tbsp) | 139 | 1.0 | 0.2 | 24 | 11 | 4.2 |
| Broad beans, boiled | 120g (4 tbsp) | 58 | 1.0 | 0.1 | 6.7 | 6.1 | 6.5 |
| Butter beans, canned, drained | 120g (4 tbsp) | 92 | 1.0 | 0.1 | 16 | 7.1 | 5.5 |
| Chickpeas, canned, drained | 120g (4 tbsp) | 138 | 3.0 | 0.4 | 19 | 8.6 | 4.9 |
| Lentils, green or brown, dried, boiled | 120g (4 tbsp) | 126 | 1.0 | 0.1 | 20 | 11 | 4.6 |
| Lentils, red, dried, boiled | 120g (4 tbsp) | 120 | 0 | 0 | 21 | 9.1 | 2.3 |
| Pinto beans, dried, boiled | 120g (4 tbsp) | 164 | 1.0 | 0.1 | 29 | 11 | * |
| Red kidney beans | 120g (4 tbsp) | 120 | 1.0 | 0.1 | 21 | 8.3 | 7.4 |
| **NUTS & SEEDS** | | | | | | | |
| Almonds | 25g (a small handful) | 153 | 14 | 1.1 | 1.7 | 5.3 | 1.9 |
| Brazil nuts | 25g (a small handful) | 171 | 17 | 4.1 | 0.8 | 3.5 | 1.1 |
| Cashew nuts | 25g (a small handful) | 143 | 12 | 2.4 | 4.5 | 4.4 | 0.8 |
| Chestnuts | 25g (a small handful) | 43 | 1.0 | 0.1 | 9.1 | 0.5 | 1.0 |
| Coconut, desiccated | 25g (a small handful) | 151 | 16 | 13 | 9.1 | 0.5 | 1.0 |
| Hazelnuts | 25g (a small handful) | 163 | 16 | 1.2 | 1.5 | 3.5 | 1.6 |
| Macadamia nuts | 25g (a small handful) | 187 | 19 | 2.8 | 1.2 | 2.0 | 1.3 |
| Peanuts, roasted, salted | 25g (a small handful) | 151 | 13 | 2.4 | 1.8 | 6.1 | 1.5 |
| Pecan nuts | 25g (a small handful) | 172 | 18 | 1.4 | 1.5 | 2.3 | 1.2 |
| Pine nuts | 25g (a small handful) | 172 | 17 | 1.1 | 1.0 | 3.5 | 0.5 |
| Pistachio nuts | 25g (a small handful) | 150 | 14 | 1.9 | 2.0 | 4.5 | 1.5 |
| Pumpkin seeds | 15g (1 tbsp) | 85 | 7.0 | 1.1 | 2.3 | 3.7 | 0.8 |
| Sesame seeds | 15g (1 tbsp) | 90 | 0 | 1.2 | 0.1 | 2.7 | 1.2 |
| Sunflower seeds | 15g (1 tbsp) | 87 | 7.0 | 0.7 | 2.8 | 3.0 | 0.9 |
| Walnuts | 25g (a small handful) | 172 | 17 | 1.4 | 0.8 | 3.7 | 0.9 |

*No information available Tr trace quantities<0.1g

| Beverages | Av Portion | Calories | Fat, g | Saturated fat, g | Carbohydrate, g | Protein, g | Fibre, g |
|---|---|---|---|---|---|---|---|
| **ALCOHOLIC DRINKS** | | | | | | | |
| Bacardi Breezer | 275ml, 1 bottle | 96 | 0 | 0 | 8.3 | 0 | 0 |
| Bailey's Original Irish Cream | 25ml, 1 measure | 82 | 3.3 | * | 6.3 | 0.8 | 0 |
| Beer, bitter, draught | 300ml, ½ pint | 96 | 0 | 0 | 6.9 | 0.9 | 0 |
| Brandy | 25ml, 1 measure | 56 | 0 | 0 | 0 | 0 | 0 |
| Champagne | 175ml, 1 glass | 133 | 0 | 0 | 2.4 | 0 | 0 |
| Cider, dry | 300ml, ½ pint | 108 | 0 | 0 | 7.8 | 0 | 0 |
| Cider, sweet | 300ml, ½ pint | 126 | 0 | 0 | 13 | 0 | 0 |
| Gin | 25ml, 1 measure | 56 | 0 | 0 | 0 | 0 | 0 |
| Guinness | 300ml, ½ pint | 90 | 0 | 0 | 4.5 | 1.2 | 0 |
| Lager | 300ml, ½ pint | 87 | 0 | 0 | 4.5 | 0.6 | 0 |
| Liqueurs, high strength e.g. Drambuie, Pernod, Cointreau, Grand Marnier | 25ml, 1 measure | 79 | 0 | 0 | 6.1 | 0 | 0 |
| Liqueurs, low–medium strength, e.g. Tia Maria, cherry brandy | 25ml, 1 measure | 66 | 0 | 0 | 8.2 | 0 | 0 |
| Port | 50ml, 1 glass | 79 | 0 | 0 | 6.0 | 0 | 0 |
| Red wine | 175ml, 1 glass | 119 | 0 | 0 | 0.4 | 0 | 0 |
| Rose wine | 175ml, 1 glass | 124 | 0 | 0 | 4.4 | 0 | 0 |
| Rum | 25ml, 1 measure | 56 | 0 | 0 | 0 | 0 | 0 |
| Sherry, dry | 50ml, 1 glass | 58 | 0 | 0 | 0.7 | 0 | 0 |
| Sherry, sweet | 50ml, 1 glass | 68 | 0 | 0 | 3.5 | 0 | 0 |
| Vermouth, dry | 50ml, 1 measure | 55 | 0 | 0 | 1.5 | 0 | 0 |
| Vermouth, sweet | 50ml, 1 measure | 76 | 0 | 0 | 7.9 | 0 | 0 |
| Vodka | 25ml, 1 measure | 56 | 0 | 0 | 0 | 0 | 0 |
| Whisky | 25ml, 1 measure | 56 | 0 | 0 | 0 | 0 | 0 |
| White wine, dry | 175ml, 1 glass | 116 | 0 | 0 | 1.1 | 0 | 0 |
| White wine, medium | 175ml, 1 glass | 130 | 0 | 0 | 5.3 | 0 | 0 |
| White wine, sparkling | 175ml, 1 glass | 130 | 0 | 0 | 8.9 | 0 | 0 |
| White wine, sweet | 175ml, 1 glass | 165 | 0 | 0 | 10 | 0 | 0 |
| **ENERGY & SPORTS DRINKS** | | | | | | | |
| Gatorade, orange | 500ml, 1 bottle | 120 | 0 | 0 | 30 | 0 | 0 |
| Lucozade energy, orange | 380ml, 1 bottle | 266 | 0 | 0 | 65 | 0 | 0 |
| Lucozade Sport Lite orange | 500ml, 1 bottle | 50 | 0 | 0 | 10 | 0 | 0 |
| Lucozade Sport orange | 500ml, 1 bottle | 140 | 0 | 0 | 32 | 0 | 0 |
| Monster energy drink | 500ml, 1 can | 228 | 0 | 0 | 57 | 0 | 0 |
| Powerade berry & tropical fruit | 500ml, 1 bottle | 80 | 0 | 0 | 20 | 0 | 0 |
| Powerade energy, berry | 500ml, 1 bottle | 220 | 0 | 0 | 53 | 0 | 0 |
| Powerade zero berry & tropical fruit | 500ml, 1 bottle | 5 | 0 | 0 | 0 | 0 | 0 |
| Red Bull | 250ml, 1 can | 113 | 0 | 0 | 28 | 0 | 0 |
| Red Bull sugar-free | 250ml, 1 can | 8 | 0 | 0 | 3.0 | 0 | 0 |
| Relentless | 500ml, 1 can | 230 | 0 | 0 | 52 | 0 | 0 |

| Beverages | Av Portion | Calories | Fat, g | Saturated fat, g | Carbohydrate, g | Protein, g | Fibre, g |
|---|---|---|---|---|---|---|---|
| **FIZZY DRINKS** | | | | | | | |
| 7 Up | 330ml, 1 can | 135 | 0 | 0 | 35 | 0 | 0 |
| 7 Up Free | 330ml, 1 can | 6 | 0 | 0 | 0.3 | 0 | 0 |
| Appletiser sparkling apple juice | 330ml bottle | 162 | 0 | 0 | 39 | 0 | 0 |
| Cola | 330ml, 1 can | 135 | 0 | 0 | 36 | 0 | 0 |
| Diet cola | 330ml, 1 can | 3 | 0 | 0 | 0 | 0 | 0 |
| Fanta orange | 330ml, 1 can | 99 | 0 | 0 | 23 | 0 | 0 |
| Fruitiser, pomegranate & raspberry | 330ml bottle | 152 | 0 | 0 | 38 | 0 | 0 |
| Ginger ale | 150ml, 1 bottle | 23 | 0 | 0 | 5.9 | 0 | 0 |
| Irn Bru | 330ml, 1 can | 142 | 0 | 0 | 35 | 0 | 0 |
| J2O, apple & mango | 330ml bottle | 142 | 0 | 0 | 33 | 0 | 0 |
| J2O, orange & passion fruit | 330ml bottle | 155 | 0 | 0 | 36 | 0 | 0 |
| Lemonade | 330ml, 1 can | 73 | 0 | 0 | 19 | 0 | 0 |
| Orangina | 330ml, 1 bottle | 139 | 0 | 0 | 33 | 0 | 0 |
| Orangina light | 330ml, 1 bottle | 20 | 0 | 0 | 4.0 | 0 | 0 |
| Schloer sparkling red grape juice | 250ml | 105 | 0 | 0 | 26 | 0 | 0 |
| Schloer sparkling white grape juice | 250ml | 105 | 0 | 0 | 26 | 0 | 0 |
| Sprite | 330ml, 1 can | 145 | 0 | 0 | 35 | 0 | 0 |
| Sprite zero | 330ml, 1 can | 3 | 0 | 0 | 0 | 0 | 0 |
| Tango apple | 330ml, 1 can | 33 | 0 | 0 | 7.0 | 0 | 0 |
| Tango orange | 330ml, 1 can | 63 | 0 | 0 | 14 | 0 | 0 |
| Tonic water | 150ml, 1 bottle | 50 | 0 | 0 | 13 | 0 | 0 |
| Vimto fizzy | 330ml, 1 can | 147 | 0 | 0 | 36 | 0 | 0 |
| **HOT DRINKS** | | | | | | | |
| Filter coffee, black | 200ml | 4 | 0 | 0 | 0.6 | 0.4 | 0 |
| Filter coffee with semi-skimmed milk | 200ml | 14 | 0.3 | 0.1 | 1.4 | 1.2 | |
| Filter coffee with whole milk | 200ml | 16 | 0.8 | 0.2 | 1.4 | 1.2 | 0 |
| Instant coffee, black | 200ml | 0 | 0 | 0 | 0 | 0 | 0 |
| Instant coffee with semi-skimmed milk | 200ml | 14 | 0.3 | 0.1 | 1.4 | 1.2 | 0 |
| Instant coffee with whole milk | 200ml | 16 | 0.8 | 0.2 | 1.4 | 1.2 | 0 |
| Green tea | 200ml | 0 | 0 | 0 | 0 | 0 | 0 |
| Herbal tea | 200ml | 2 | 0 | 0 | 0.4 | 0 | 0 |
| Tea with semi-skimmed milk | 200ml | 14 | 0.3 | 0.1 | 1.4 | 1.2 | 0 |
| Tea with whole milk | 200ml | 16 | 0.8 | 0.2 | 1.4 | 1.2 | 0 |
| Hot chocolate with semi-skimmed milk | 200ml | 146 | 4.0 | 2.5 | 1.4 | 1.0 | 0 |
| Hot chocolate with whole milk | 200ml | 180 | 8.0 | 5.2 | 21 | 7.0 | 0 |
| Cocoa with semi-skimmed milk | 200ml | 114 | 4.0 | 2.4 | 14 | 7.0 | 0 |
| Cocoa with whole milk | 200ml | 152 | 8.0 | 5.2 | 14 | 6.8 | 0 |
| Latte with semi-skimmed milk | 200ml | 143 | 5.1 | 2.6 | 15 | 9.5 | 0 |
| Latte with whole milk | 200ml | 172 | 8.4 | 4.8 | 15 | 9.1 | 0 |
| Cappuccino with semi-skimmed milk | 200ml | 97 | 3.4 | 1.7 | 10 | 6.4 | 0 |
| Cappuccino with whole milk | 200ml | 116 | 5.6 | 3.2 | 10 | 6.1 | 0 |
| Mocha with semi-skimmed milk and whipped cream | 200ml | 273 | 13 | 7.7 | 33 | 9.8 | 0 |
| Mocha with whole milk and whipped cream | 200ml | 297 | 16 | 9.5 | 33 | 9.5 | 0 |

*No information available  Tr trace quantities<0.1g

| Biscuits (savoury) & cereal bars | Av Portion | Calories | Fat, g | Saturated fat, g | Carbohydrate, g | Protein, g | Fibre, g |
|---|---|---|---|---|---|---|---|
| **SAVOURY BISCUITS** | | | | | | | |
| Carr's table water biscuits | Each | 14 | 0.3 | 0.1 | 2.5 | 0.3 | 0.1 |
| Jacob's cream crackers | Each | 34 | 1.1 | 0.4 | 5.4 | 0.8 | 0.3 |
| Nairn's oatcakes | Each | 45 | 2.0 | 0.5 | 5.7 | 1.1 | 1.1 |
| Ryvita crackers, golden rye | Each | 27 | 0.2 | Tr | 5.1 | 0.9 | 0.5 |
| Ryvita multigrain crispbread | Each | 37 | 0.6 | 0.1 | 6.7 | 1.1 | 1.8 |
| Ryvita rye crispbread | Each | 32 | 0.2 | Tr | 6.7 | 0.9 | 1.7 |
| Ryvita wholegrain crackerbread | Each | 20 | 0.2 | Tr | 3.9 | 0.7 | 0.6 |
| Snack-a-Jacks Jumbo, cheese | Each | 38 | 0.3 | 0.1 | 8.1 | 0.9 | 0.2 |
| Tuc snack cracker | Each | 24 | 1.3 | 1.0 | 2.6 | 0.3 | 0.1 |
| **CEREAL BARS** | | | | | | | |
| Alpen fruit & nut bars, milk chocolate | Each | 125 | 3.9 | 1.7 | 20 | 2.1 | 0.5 |
| Eat Natural, almond, apricot & yogurt | Each | 228 | 12 | 8.2 | 26 | 2.9 | 2.9 |
| Jordan's Absolute Nut bar | Each | 243 | 18 | 1.7 | 16 | 5.0 | 2.9 |
| Jordan's Crunchy bar, honey & almond | Each | 139 | 6.8 | 0.9 | 17 | 2.5 | 2.0 |
| Jordan's Frusli bar, raisin & hazelnut | Each | 117 | 3.7 | 0.5 | 19 | 1.7 | 1.4 |
| Kellogg's Coco Pops snack bar | Each | 85 | 2.5 | 2.0 | 14 | 1.5 | 0.2 |
| Kellogg's Elevenses chocolate chip oat cookies | Each | 181 | 8.0 | 3.0 | 24 | 2.5 | 1.5 |
| Kellogg's Frosties snack bar | Each | 103 | 3.0 | 2.0 | 18 | 2.0 | 0.3 |
| Kellogg's Nutrigrain, strawberry | Each | 133 | 3.0 | 1.0 | 26 | 1.5 | 1.5 |
| Kellogg's Rice Krispies squares, marshmallow | Each | 118 | 3.5 | 2.0 | 21 | 0.8 | 0.3 |
| McVitie's Go Ahead fruit bakes, cherry | Each | 131 | 3.0 | 1.0 | 26 | 1.5 | 1.5 |
| McVitie's Go Ahead yogurt breaks, raspberry | Each | 72 | 1.8 | 0.8 | 13 | 1.0 | 0.4 |
| Nature Valley crunchy granola bars, Canadian maple syrup | Each | 191 | 6.9 | 0.8 | 27 | 3.4 | 2.5 |
| Special K Bliss bar, chocolate & raspberry | Each | 89 | 2.0 | 1.0 | 16 | 0.9 | 0.9 |
| Special K Mini Breaks | Each | 99 | 2.5 | 0.8 | 17 | 2.0 | 0.8 |

| Biscuits (sweet) & bars | Av Portion | Calories | Fat, g | Saturated fat, g | Carbohydrate, g | Protein, g | Fibre, g |
|---|---|---|---|---|---|---|---|
| **SWEET BISCUITS** | | | | | | | |
| Bourbon Creams | Each | 67 | 3.0 | 1.8 | 9.3 | 0.8 | 0.5 |
| Cadbury Dairy Milk biscuits | Each | 75 | 4.3 | 2.5 | 8.4 | 1.1 | 0.2 |
| Cadbury milk chocolate fingers | Each | 30 | 1.5 | 0.6 | 3.4 | 0.4 | Tr |
| Chocolate chip cookies | Each | 57 | 2.6 | 1.4 | 7.4 | 0.7 | 0.1 |
| Chocolate Hobnobs | Each | 92 | 4.5 | 2.2 | 12 | 1.3 | 0.9 |
| Custard creams | Each | 65 | 2.7 | 1.4 | 8.8 | 0.7 | 0.2 |
| Digestives | Each | 70 | 3.1 | 0.7 | 9.3 | 1.1 | 0.5 |
| Digestives, light | Each | 66 | 2.4 | 1.1 | 10 | 1.1 | 0.5 |
| Fig rolls | Each | 63 | 1.5 | 0.7 | 12 | 0.7 | 0.6 |
| Garibaldi | Each | 40 | 0.9 | 0.4 | 7.4 | 0.5 | 0.2 |
| Ginger nuts | Each | 53 | 1.9 | 0.9 | 8.3 | 0.6 | 0.3 |
| Hobnobs | Each | 67 | 3.1 | 0.7 | 8.7 | 1.0 | 0.8 |
| Jaffa cakes | Each | 46 | 1.0 | 0.5 | 8.7 | 0.6 | 0.3 |
| Jam sandwich creams | Each | 75 | 3.4 | 2.0 | 10 | 0.7 | 0.3 |
| Jammie dodgers | Each | 83 | 2.8 | 1.3 | 13 | 1.0 | 0.3 |
| Milk chocolate digestives | Each | 84 | 4.0 | 2.1 | 11 | 1.2 | 0.5 |
| Rich tea | Each | 38 | 1.3 | 0.3 | 5.9 | 0.6 | 0.2 |
| Shortbread fingers | Each | 95 | 5.3 | 3.4 | 11 | 1.2 | 0.5 |
| **BARS** | | | | | | | |
| Blue Ribband | Each | 99 | 4.9 | 3.1 | 13 | 0.9 | 0.2 |
| Club, orange | Each | 112 | 5.9 | 3.7 | 13 | 1.1 | 0.5 |
| Fabulous Baking Boys flapjack | 75g bar | 346 | 16 | 6.9 | 46 | 5.1 | 2.8 |
| Penguin bar | Each | 114 | 6.1 | 3.4 | 14 | 1.2 | 0.5 |

| Bread & bakery | Av Portion | Calories | Fat, g | Saturated fat, g | Carbohydrate, g | Protein, g | Fibre, g |
|---|---|---|---|---|---|---|---|
| Bagel, plain | 85g | 232 | 1.8 | * | 49 | 8.5 | 2.0 |
| Brioche roll | 35g | 129 | 4.6 | 3.0 | 19 | 2.8 | 0.7 |
| Brown bread, sliced | 1 slice, 40g | 85 | 1.6 | * | 18 | 3.2 | 1.4 |
| Burger bun | 85g | 224 | 4.0 | 0.9 | 42 | 7.7 | 1.3 |
| Chapatti | 55g | 111 | 1.0 | 0.1 | 24 | 4.0 | * |
| Ciabatta bread | 1 slice, 30g | 92 | 2.1 | 0.4 | 16 | 3.0 | 0.7 |
| Croissant | 40g | 186 | 12 | 7.0 | 16 | 3.2 | 1.0 |
| Crumpet | 40g | 77 | 0.4 | Tr | 16 | 2.4 | 0.9 |
| French stick | 1 slice, 40g | 105 | 1.0 | 0.1 | 22 | 3.6 | 1.0 |
| Garlic bread | 1 slice, 30g | 110 | 5.0 | 2.9 | 14 | 2.3 | * |
| Hovis Best of Both | 1 slice, 40g | 86 | 0.7 | 0.2 | 16 | 3.6 | 2.0 |
| Hovis Seed Sensation | 1 slice, 44g | 122 | 2.9 | 0.3 | 19 | 4.4 | 2.3 |
| Muffin, plain | 67g | 174 | 4.7 | 2.3 | 26 | 7.0 | 1.6 |
| Naan bread | 160g | 456 | 12 | 1.6 | 80 | 13 | 3.2 |
| Pitta bread, white | 60g | 153 | 1.0 | 0.1 | 33 | 5.5 | 1.4 |
| Pitta bread, wholemeal | 60g | 159 | 0.7 | * | 35 | 5.5 | 3.1 |
| Rye bread | 1 slice, 40g | 88 | 1.0 | 0.1 | 18 | 3.3 | 1.8 |
| Scotch pancake (Kingsmill) | 28g | 74 | 1.2 | 0.2 | 14 | 1.5 | 0.4 |
| Soda bread | 1 slice, 40g | 103 | 1.0 | * | 22 | 3.1 | 0.8 |
| Tortilla, plain | 55g | 144 | 1.0 | * | 33 | 4.0 | 1.3 |
| White bread, sliced | 1 slice, 40g | 88 | 1.0 | 0.1 | 18 | 3.2 | 0.8 |
| White roll, crusty | 50g | 131 | 1.0 | 0.3 | 28 | 4.6 | 1.2 |
| White roll, soft | 50g | 127 | 1.0 | 0.3 | 26 | 4.7 | 1.0 |
| Wholemeal bread, sliced | 1 slice, 40g | 87 | 1.0 | 0.2 | 18 | 3.2 | 0.8 |
| Wholemeal roll | 50g | 122 | 2.0 | 0.4 | 23 | 5.2 | 2.2 |
| Wrap | 64g | 182 | 3.2 | 1.4 | 32 | 5.3 | 2.4 |

| Breakfast cereals | Av Portion | Calories | Fat, g | Saturated fat, g | Carbohydrate, g | Protein, g | Fibre, g |
|---|---|---|---|---|---|---|---|
| All Bran, Kellogg's | 30g | 100 | 1.1 | 0.2 | 14 | 4.2 | 8.1 |
| Alpen high fibre | 45g | 154 | 3.2 | 0.4 | 28 | 3.5 | 6.3 |
| Alpen original | 45g | 170 | 2.6 | 0.4 | 30 | 5.0 | 3.2 |
| Bitesize Shredded Wheat | 45g | 155 | 1.0 | 0.2 | 32 | 5.4 | 5.4 |
| Bran Flakes, Kellogg's | 30g | 107 | 0.6 | 0.2 | 20 | 3.0 | 4.5 |
| Cheerios | 30g | 114 | 3.2 | 1.5 | 23 | 2.6 | 2.1 |
| Choco Cornflakes, Kellogg's | 30g | 117 | 0.9 | 0.5 | 25 | 1.5 | 0.9 |
| Clusters | 30g | 116 | 1.5 | 0.5 | 22 | 2.7 | 2.2 |
| Coco Pops | 30g | 116 | 0.8 | 0.3 | 26 | 1.5 | 0.6 |
| Cookie Crisp | 30g | 115 | 0.9 | 0.3 | 24 | 2.0 | 1.5 |
| Cornflakes, Kellogg's | 30g | 113 | 0.3 | 0.1 | 25 | 2.1 | 0.9 |
| Country Crisp, raisin | 50g | 206 | 6.7 | 1.8 | 33 | 3.4 | 2.9 |
| Country Crisp, strawberry | 50g | 218 | 8.0 | 2.3 | 33 | 3.9 | 3.5 |
| Crunchy Bran, Weetabix | 40g | 140 | 1.4 | 0.2 | 23 | 4.8 | 8.0 |
| Crunchy Nut Cornflakes, Kellogg's | 30g | 121 | 1.5 | 0.3 | 25 | 1.8 | 0.8 |
| Curiously Cinnamon | 30g | 126 | 3.0 | 1.1 | 23 | 1.5 | 1.2 |
| Frosted Wheats | 40g | 146 | 0.8 | 0.1 | 29 | 4.0 | 3.6 |
| Frosties | 30g | 113 | 0.2 | Tr | 26 | 1.4 | 0.6 |
| Fruit 'n' Fibre | 30g | 114 | 1.8 | 1.1 | 21 | 2.4 | 2.7 |
| Golden Grahams | 30g | 115 | 0.9 | 0.3 | 24 | 2.0 | 1.4 |
| Golden Nuggets | 30g | 113 | 0.4 | 0.1 | 25 | 2.2 | 1.1 |
| Granola, Quaker Oats | 50g | 205 | 4.4 | 1.4 | 37 | 4.3 | 2.6 |
| Harvest Crunch, fruity raisins | 45g | 200 | 6.8 | 0.7 | 30 | 3.2 | 2.9 |
| Honey Loops | 30g | 113 | 0.9 | 0.2 | 23 | 2.4 | 2.1 |
| Honey Nut Shredded Wheat | 40g | 151 | 2.6 | 0.9 | 28 | 4.4 | 3.8 |
| Hot Oat Crumbly, original | 45g | 217 | 9.9 | 5.0 | 27 | 3.6 | 2.7 |
| Krave, chocolate hazelnut | 30g | 134 | 4.8 | 1.8 | 20 | 2.4 | 1.2 |
| Muesli, Jordan's fruit & nut | 45g | 216 | 5.5 | 2.3 | 32 | 7.8 | 3.2 |
| Muesli, Jordan's natural | 50g | 210 | 4.1 | 1.5 | 35 | 8.0 | 4.7 |
| Nesquik | 30g | 116 | 1.2 | 0.5 | 23 | 2.3 | 2.0 |
| Oat So Simple | 27g (1 sachet) | 103 | 2.3 | 0.4 | 16 | 3.0 | 2.5 |
| Oatibix | 48g (2 biscuits) | 189 | 3.8 | 0.6 | 31 | 6.0 | 3.5 |
| Oatibix Bites | 40g | 158 | 2.9 | 0.4 | 27 | 4.2 | 4.0 |
| Oatibix Flakes | 30g | 119 | 2.0 | 0.3 | 22 | 2.9 | 2.2 |
| Oats & More, honey | 40g | 150 | 2.0 | 0.4 | 29 | 3.9 | 2.5 |
| Oats, Quaker | 40g | 142 | 3.2 | 0.6 | 24 | 4.4 | 3.6 |
| Optivita, raisin | 30g | 109 | 1.4 | 0.2 | 20 | 2.7 | 2.4 |
| Ready Brek, original | 30g | 112 | 2.6 | 0.4 | 17 | 3.5 | 2.4 |
| Rice Krispies | 30g | 115 | 0.3 | Tr | 27 | 1.4 | 0.2 |

| Breakfast cereals | Av Portion | Calories | Fat, g | Saturated fat, g | Carbohydrate, g | Protein, g | Fibre, g |
|---|---|---|---|---|---|---|---|
| Ricicles | 30g | 115 | 0.2 | Tr | 27 | 1.4 | 0.2 |
| Shredded Wheat | 45g | 153 | 2.8 | 0.3 | 31 | 5.2 | 5.3 |
| Shreddies | 40g | 148 | 0.8 | 0.2 | 30 | 4.0 | 4.0 |
| Special K | 30g | 114 | 0.5 | 0.2 | 23 | 4.2 | 0.8 |
| Special K clusters, honey | 30g | 117 | 0.9 | 0.2 | 24 | 2.7 | 1.2 |
| Special K fruit & nut | 30g | 114 | 0.8 | 0.1 | 23 | 3.6 | 0.8 |
| Special K strawberry & chocolate | 30g | 116 | 0.9 | 0.3 | 23 | 3.6 | 0.9 |
| Start | 30g | 117 | 1.1 | 0.6 | 24 | 2.4 | 1.5 |
| Weetabix | 37.5g (2 biscuits) | 134 | 0.8 | 0.2 | 26 | 4.3 | 3.8 |
| Weetabix Mini, chocolate chip | 40g | 155 | 2.1 | 1.0 | 28 | 3.8 | 3.8 |
| Weetos | 30g | 118 | 1.5 | 0.3 | 23 | 2.5 | 1.9 |

| Cakes, pastries & buns | Av Portion | Calories | Fat, g | Saturated fat, g | Carbohydrate, g | Protein, g | Fibre, g |
|---|---|---|---|---|---|---|---|
| Battenburg cake | | | | | | | |
| Carrot cake | 75g slice | 269 | 17 | 4.1 | 28 | 3.2 | 0.8 |
| Chocolate cake | 75g slice | 342 | 20 | * | 38 | 5.6 | * |
| Chocolate fudge cake | 75g slice | 269 | 11 | 3.4 | 42 | 3.9 | 0.7 |
| Chocolate roll | 30g each | 116 | 5.0 | 2.1 | 17 | 1.3 | * |
| Cream horn | 60g each | 261 | 21 | 10 | 16 | 2.3 | 0.5 |
| Currant bun | 60g each | 168 | 3.0 | 1.1 | 32 | 4.8 | 1.3 |
| Custard tart | 90g each | 249 | 13 | 5.5 | 29 | 5.7 | 1.1 |
| Danish pastry | 110g each | 376 | 16 | 9.4 | 56 | 6.4 | 1.8 |
| Doughnut, iced | 75g each | 287 | 13 | * | 41 | 3.6 | * |
| Doughnut, jam | 75g each | 252 | 11 | 3.2 | 37 | 4.3 | * |
| Éclair | 40g each | 149 | 10 | * | 15 | 1.6 | 0.2 |
| Fruit cake | 60g slice | 223 | 9.0 | 4.1 | 35 | 3.1 | * |
| Fruit cake, iced | 70g slice | 245 | 7.0 | 1.2 | 46 | 2.5 | 0.9 |
| Fruit scone | 60g each | 189 | 5.0 | 1.4 | 34 | 3.9 | 1.2 |
| Gingerbread | 50g slice | 190 | 6.0 | * | 32 | 2.8 | 0.6 |
| Hot cross bun | 70g each | 218 | 5.0 | 1.3 | 41 | 5.2 | 1.3 |
| Iced cup cake | 40g each | 142 | 4.0 | 1.3 | 28 | 1.5 | * |
| Jam tart | 40g each | 153 | 6.0 | 2.7 | 25 | 1.3 | * |
| Madeira cake | 75g slice | 283 | 11 | 6.3 | 44 | 4.1 | 0.7 |
| Mince pie | 55g each | 239 | 12 | * | 33 | 2.3 | 1.0 |
| Scone, plain | 60g each | 218 | 9.0 | 2.2 | 32 | 4.3 | 1.1 |
| Sponge cake, cream & jam | 60g slice | 168 | 7.0 | * | 26 | 2.6 | 0 |
| Sponge cake, jam | 60g slice | 181 | 3.0 | 1.0 | 39 | 2.5 | 1.1 |
| Swiss roll | 30g slice | 83 | 1.0 | * | 17 | 2.2 | 0.2 |
| Teacake | 60g each | 178 | 3.0 | * | 32 | 4.8 | * |

| Cheese, cream, milk & yogurt | Av Portion | Calories | Fat, g | Saturated fat, g | Carbohydrate, g | Protein, g | Fibre, g |
|---|---|---|---|---|---|---|---|
| **CHEESE** | | | | | | | |
| Babybel | 20g (1 mini) | 63 | 5.0 | * | 0 | 4.5 | 0 |
| Blue Stilton | 40g | 164 | 14 | 9.2 | 0 | 9.5 | 0 |
| Brie | 40g | 137 | 12 | 7.3 | 0 | 8.1 | 0 |
| Camembert | 40g | 116 | 9.0 | 5.7 | 0 | 8.6 | 0 |
| Cheddar | 40g | 166 | 14 | 8.7 | 0 | 10 | 0 |
| Cheddar, half fat | 40g | 109 | 6.0 | 4.0 | 0 | 13 | 0 |
| Cheestrings | 21g (1 cheestring) | 69 | 5.0 | 3.1 | 0 | 5.9 | 0 |
| Cheshire | 40g | 152 | 13 | 7.8 | 0 | 9.6 | 0 |
| Cottage cheese | 40g | 40 | 2.0 | 0.9 | 1.2 | 5.0 | 0 |
| Cream cheese | 30g (1 tbsp) | 132 | 14 | 8.9 | 0 | 0.9 | 0 |
| Danish blue | 40g | 137 | 12 | 7.7 | 0 | 8.2 | 0 |
| Double Gloucester | 40g | 162 | 14 | 8.5 | 0 | 9.8 | 0 |
| Edam | 40g | 136 | 10 | 6.3 | 0 | 11 | 0 |
| Emmental | 40g | 153 | 12 | 7.4 | 0 | 12 | 0 |
| Feta | 40g | 100 | 8.0 | 5.5 | 0.6 | 6.2 | 0 |
| Goat's cheese | 40g | 128 | 101 | 7.2 | 0.4 | 8.4 | 0 |
| Gouda | 40g | 151 | 12 | 8.1 | 0 | 10 | 0 |
| Gruyère | 40g | 164 | 13 | 8.3 | 0 | 11 | 0 |
| Mozzarella | 40g | 103 | 8.0 | 5.5 | 0 | 7.4 | 0 |
| Parmesan | 10g (1 tbsp) | 42 | 3.0 | 1.9 | 0.1 | 3.6 | 0 |
| Philadelphia | 30g (1 tbsp) | 74 | 7.0 | 4.1 | 0.9 | 1.7 | 0.1 |
| Philadelphia light | 30g (1 tbsp) | 47 | 3.5 | 2.3 | 1.2 | 2.5 | 0.1 |
| Processed cheese | 20g (1 slice) | 59 | 5.0 | 2.9 | 1.0 | 3.6 | 0 |
| Red Leicester | 40g | 160 | 13 | 8.4 | 0 | 9.7 | 0 |
| Ricotta | 40g | 58 | 4.0 | 2.8 | 0.8 | 0.8 | 0 |
| Wensleydale | 40g | 151 | 13 | 7.9 | 0 | 9.3 | 0 |
| **CREAM** | | | | | | | |
| Clotted | 30g (1 tbsp) | 176 | 19 | 12 | 0.7 | 0.5 | 0 |
| Crème fraiche | 30g (1 tbsp) | 113 | 12 | 8.1 | 0.7 | 0.7 | 0 |
| Crème fraiche, half-fat | 30g (1 tbsp) | 49 | 5.0 | 3.0 | 1.3 | 0.8 | 0 |
| Double | 30g (1 tbsp) | 149 | 16 | 10 | 0.5 | 0.5 | 0 |
| Single | 30g (1 tbsp) | 58 | 6.0 | 3.6 | 0.7 | 1.0 | 0 |
| Whipping | 30g (1 tbsp) | 114 | 12 | 7.6 | 0.8 | 0.6 | 0 |

| Cheese, cream, milk & yogurt | Av Portion | Calories | Fat, g | Saturated fat, g | Carbohydrate, g | Protein, g | Fibre, g |
|---|---|---|---|---|---|---|---|
| **MILK** | | | | | | | |
| Alpro soya milk alternative, original | 100ml | 43 | 1.9 | 0.3 | 2.9 | 3.3 | 0.6 |
| Channel Island milk, whole | 100ml | 78 | 5.0 | 3.3 | 4.8 | 3.6 | 0 |
| Coconut milk, Amoy | 100ml | 165 | 17 | 14 | 2.0 | 1.0 | 1.0 |
| Coconut milk, reduced fat, Amoy | 100ml | 110 | 11 | 9.0 | 2.0 | 1.0 | 1.0 |
| Condensed milk, skimmed, sweetened | 100ml | 267 | 0.2 | 0.1 | 60 | 10 | 0 |
| Condensed milk, whole, sweetened | 100ml | 333 | 10 | 6.3 | 56 | 8.5 | 0 |
| EcoMil almond organic milk alternative | 100ml | 46 | 2.1 | 0.2 | 5.4 | 0.9 | 0.8 |
| Evaporated milk | 100ml | 151 | 9.0 | 5.9 | 8.5 | 8.4 | 0 |
| Evaporated milk, light | 100ml | 123 | 4.0 | 2.7 | 13 | 9.2 | 0 |
| Flavoured milk | 100ml | 64 | 2.0 | 1.0 | 9.6 | 3.6 | 0 |
| Goat's milk | 100ml | 64 | 4.0 | 2.4 | 4.4 | 3.1 | 0 |
| Hot chocolate, made with semi-skimmed milk | 100ml | 73 | 2.0 | 1.3 | 11 | 3.6 | 0 |
| Lactofree, semi-skimmed | 100ml | 40 | 1.7 | 1.1 | 2.6 | 3.2 | 0 |
| Oatly organic oat drink | 100ml | 35 | 0.7 | 0.1 | 6.5 | 1.0 | 0.8 |
| Rice Dream organic milk alternative | 100ml | 4 | 1.0 | 0.1 | 9.4 | 0.1 | 0.1 |
| Semi-skimmed milk | 100ml | 46 | 2.0 | 1.1 | 4.7 | 3.5 | 0 |
| Skimmed milk | 100ml | 34 | 0.1 | Tr | 4.8 | 3.5 | 0 |
| Whole milk | 100ml | 66 | 4.0 | 2.5 | 4.6 | 3.3 | 0 |
| **YOGURT** | | | | | | | |
| Alpro soya yogurt, plain | 100g (1 pot) | 46 | 2.3 | 0.4 | 2.1 | 4.0 | 1.0 |
| Danone Actimel drink, strawberry | 100g (1 bottle) | 75 | 1.5 | 1.1 | 12 | 2.7 | 0 |
| Danone Activia 0%, raspberry | 125g (1 pot) | 59 | 0.1 | 0 | 8.6 | 5.8 | 3.1 |
| Danone Activia creamy, strawberry | 120g (1 pot) | 117 | 3.6 | 2.3 | 15 | 5.8 | 0.2 |
| Danone Activia pouring yogurt, vanilla | 130g | 81 | 2.1 | 1.3 | 11 | 5.1 | 0 |
| Danone Activia, strawberry | 125g (1 pot) | 116 | 4.0 | 2.5 | 16 | 4.4 | 2.5 |
| Fat-free yogurt, fruit | 125g (1 pot) | 59 | 0 | 0 | 8.8 | 6.0 | 0 |
| Fat-free yogurt, plain | 125g (1 pot) | 68 | 0 | 0 | 10 | 6.8 | 0 |
| Greek-style yogurt, fruit | 125g (1 pot) | 171 | 10 | 7.0 | 14 | 6.0 | 0 |
| Greek-style yogurt, plain | 125g (1 pot) | 166 | 13 | 8.4 | 6.0 | 7.1 | 0 |
| Low-fat yogurt, fruit | 125g (1 pot) | 98 | 1.0 | 1.0 | 17 | 5.2 | 0.3 |
| Low-fat yogurt, plain | 125g (1 pot) | 70 | 1.0 | 0.8 | 9.3 | 6.0 | 0 |
| Müller Corner greek yogurt, black cherry | 150g (1 pot) | 173 | 4.5 | 2.7 | 24 | 7.5 | 0.2 |
| Müller Light, strawberry | 175g (1 pot) | 89 | 0.2 | 0.2 | 14 | 6.8 | 0.4 |
| Müller Vitality yogurt drink, raspberry | 100g (1 bottle) | 74 | 1.7 | 1.0 | 11 | 2.8 | 1.0 |
| Whole milk yogurt, fruit | 150g (1 pot) | 164 | 5.0 | 3.0 | 27 | 6.0 | 0 |
| Whole milk, yogurt, plain | 150g (1 pot) | 119 | 5.0 | 2.6 | 12 | 8.5 | 0 |
| Yakult fermented milk drink | 65g (1 bottle) | 43 | 0 | 0 | 9.6 | 0.9 | 0 |
| Yeo Valley organic yogurt pots, strawberry | 120g (1 pot) | 123 | 4.4 | 2.8 | 15 | 5.8 | 0.1 |

| Confectionery & ice cream | Av Portion | Calories | Fat, g | Saturated fat, g | Carbohydrate, g | Protein, g | Fibre, g |
|---|---|---|---|---|---|---|---|
| Aero, peppermint chunky bar | 1 bar | 157 | 8.9 | 5.1 | 18 | 1.5 | 0.3 |
| Boiled sweets | 25g | 82 | 0 | 0 | 22 | 0 | 0 |
| Boost | 1 bar | 310 | 17 | 13 | 35 | 3.5 | 0.5 |
| Bounty twin bar | 57g, 1 twin bar | 268 | 14 | 12 | 33 | 2.4 | 1.0 |
| Bournville plain chocolate | 45g, 1 bar | 225 | 12 | 7.5 | 27 | 2.1 | 0.9 |
| Buttons, Cadbury's | 33g, 1 pack | 170 | 9.6 | 6.0 | 18 | 2.4 | 0.2 |
| Celebrations | 100g | 492 | 24 | 14 | 62 | 5.6 | 1.2 |
| Chocolate orange, milk chocolate | 26g, 3 segments | 138 | 7.8 | 4.6 | 15 | 1.9 | 0.5 |
| Chocolate, milk | 50g | 260 | 15 | 9.1 | 29 | 3.8 | 0.4 |
| Chocolate, plain | 50g | 255 | 14 | 8.4 | 32 | 2.5 | 1.3 |
| Chocolate, white | 50g | 265 | 15 | 9.2 | 29 | 4.0 | * |
| Creme egg | Each | 180 | 6.3 | 3.9 | 29 | 1.6 | 0.2 |
| Crunchie | 1 bar | 185 | 7.6 | 4.9 | 28 | 1.4 | 0.5 |
| Dairy Milk bar | 49g, 1 bar | 260 | 15 | 9.1 | 28 | 3.7 | 0.3 |
| Dairy Milk bar, fruit & nut | 49g, 1 bar | 240 | 13 | 7.1 | 27 | 4.1 | 0.7 |
| Double Decker | 1 bar | 275 | 11 | 7.4 | 41 | 2.6 | 0.8 |
| Flake | 1 bar | 170 | 9.9 | 6.1 | 18 | 2.6 | 0.2 |
| Fruit gums | 25g | 81 | 0 | 0 | 20 | 1.6 | * |
| Fruit pastilles | 1 tube | 187 | 0 | 0 | 45 | 2.3 | 0 |
| Fudge | 25g | 110 | 3.0 | 2.2 | 20 | 0.8 | 0 |
| Fudge bar | 1 bar | 110 | 3.9 | 2.2 | 19 | 0.6 | 0.1 |
| Galaxy | 46g, 1 bar | 250 | 15 | 8.9 | 26 | 3.0 | 0.7 |
| Jelly Beans | 25g | 95 | Tr | Tr | 23 | Tr | Tr |
| Kit Kat | 4 fingers | 233 | 12 | 7.2 | 29 | 2.7 | 0.9 |
| Lion bar | 1 bar | 277 | 14 | 8.6 | 26 | 2.6 | 1.0 |
| Liquorice Allsorts | 25g | 87 | 1.0 | 0.9 | 19 | 0.9 | 0.5 |
| M&Ms, peanut | 45g, 1 bag | 228 | 11 | 4.5 | 27 | 4.2 | 1.2 |
| Maltesers | 37g, 1 bag | 187 | 9.2 | 5.6 | 23 | 3.0 | 0.4 |
| Mars bar | 58g, 1 bar | 260 | 9.9 | 4.8 | 40 | 2.5 | 0.7 |
| Milk Tray | 100g | 485 | 24 | 13 | 64 | 3.9 | 1.3 |
| Milky Bar | 1 bar | 136 | 7.9 | 4.7 | 14 | 1.9 | 0 |
| Milky Way | 22g, 1 bar | 98 | 3.5 | 1.7 | 16 | 0.9 | 0.1 |
| Mint imperials | 1 sweet | 10 | - | - | 2.4 | 0 | 0 |
| Peppermints | 25g | 98 | 0 | 0 | 26 | 0.1 | 0 |
| Polo mints | 1 tube | 139 | 0.4 | 0.4 | 34 | Tr | 0 |
| Quality Street | 3 sweets | 133 | 5.8 | 3.4 | 19 | 1.0 | 0.4 |
| Roses | 100g | 495 | 25 | 14 | 62 | 4.5 | 0.6 |
| Smarties | 1 tube | 91 | 3.4 | 1.9 | 14 | 0.8 | 0.5 |
| Snickers | 58g, 1 bar | 296 | 16 | 5.5 | 32 | 5.5 | 0.8 |
| Time Out | 1 bar | 170 | 9.7 | 6.3 | 18 | 2.3 | 0.4 |
| Toffees | 24g, 3 sweets | 110 | 4.3 | 2.4 | 18 | 0.4 | 0.1 |
| Twirl | 1 bar | 230 | 13 | 8.2 | 24 | 3.3 | 0.3 |
| Twix | 58g, 2 fingers | 286 | 14 | 8.0 | 37 | 2.8 | 0.8 |
| Walnut whip | Each | 174 | 8.9 | 4.9 | 22 | 1.9 | 0.2 |
| Wine gums | 25g | 81 | Tr | Tr | 19 | 0.9 | Tr |

*No information available Tr trace quantities<0.1g

| Confectionery & ice cream | Av Portion | Calories | Fat, g | Saturated fat, g | Carbohydrate, g | Protein, g | Fibre, g |
|---|---|---|---|---|---|---|---|
| Wispa | 1 bar | 215 | 13 | 8.3 | 21 | 2.8 | 0.3 |
| Yorkie, original milk | 1 bar | 302 | 17 | 10 | 32 | 3.4 | 1.0 |
| **ICE CREAM** | | | | | | | |
| Dairy ice cream, flavoured | 75g, 2 scoops | 134 | 6.0 | 3.9 | 19 | 2.6 | 0 |
| Dairy ice cream, vanilla | 75g, 2 scoops | 133 | 7.0 | 4.6 | 15 | 2.7 | 0 |
| Ice cream cone | Each, 75g | 140 | 6.0 | * | 19 | 2.6 | 0 |
| Non-dairy ice cream, flavoured | 75g 2 scoops | 125 | 6.0 | 2.8 | 17 | 2.3 | 0 |
| Non-dairy ice cream, vanilla | 75g 2 scoops | 115 | 6.0 | 3.6 | 14 | 2.3 | 0 |
| Sorbet, fruit | 75g, 2 scoops | 73 | 0 | 0 | 19 | 0.2 | 0 |
| Ben & Jerry's caramel chew chew ice cream | 100ml, 2 scoops | 240 | 14 | 9 | 26 | 3.5 | 0.5 |
| Ben & Jerry's cherry garcia frozen yogurt | 100ml, 2 scoops | 140 | 2.5 | 2 | 26 | 3.5 | 0.6 |
| Ben & Jerry's chocolate fudge brownie frozen yogurt | 100ml, | 150 | 2 | 1 | 29 | 4.5 | 1 |
| Ben & Jerry's chocolate fudge brownie ice cream | 100ml, 2 scoops | 210 | 10 | 7 | 25 | 4 | 1.5 |
| Ben & Jerry's cookie dough ice cream | 100ml, 2 scoops | 210 | 12 | 7 | 23 | 3 | 0.5 |
| Ben & Jerry's phish food ice cream | 100ml, 2 scoops | 230 | 11 | 8 | 30 | 3 | 1.5 |
| Cadbury's Dairy Milk ice cream bar | 100ml, 1 bar | 235 | 15 | * | 25 | 3.0 | * |
| Carte d'Or chocolate inspiration ice cream | 100ml, 2 scoops | 110 | 5.0 | * | 15 | 2.0 | * |
| Carte d'Or light vanilla ice cream | 100ml, 2 scoops | 70 | 2.0 | 2.0 | 11 | 1.0 | 2.0 |
| Carte d'Or rum & raisin ice cream | 100ml, 2 scoops | 100 | 4.0 | * | 12 | 1.5 | * |
| Carte d'Or vanilla ice cream | 100ml, 2 scoops | 100 | 4.5 | * | 14 | 1.5 | * |
| Cornetto classico | 90ml, 1 cone | 180 | 10 | 8.0 | 20 | 2.5 | 0.9 |
| Cornetto strawberry | 90ml, 1 cone | 140 | 5.0 | 4.0 | 23 | 1.5 | 0.6 |
| Del Monte raspberry iced smoothie | 90ml, 1 stick | 85 | Tr | Tr | 21 | 0.3 | 0.7 |
| Green & Black's vanilla ice cream | 145ml, 3 scoops | 219 | 13 | 8.0 | 20 | 4.5 | 0.1 |
| Green & Black's chocolate ice cream | 145ml, 3 scoops | 248 | 14 | 8.7 | 25 | 5.0 | 1.1 |
| Haagan Dazs cookies & cream ice cream | 100ml, 1 mini tub | 225 | 14 | * | 20 | 3.7 | * |
| Haagan Dazs pralines & cream ice cream | 100ml, 1 mini tub | 245 | 15 | * | 25 | 3.6 | * |
| Haagan Dazs strawberry cheesecake ice cream | 100ml, 1 mini tub | 236 | 14 | * | 25 | 3.3 | * |
| Haagan Dazs vanilla ice cream | 100ml, 1 mini tub | 225 | 15 | * | 18 | 3.8 | * |
| Kelly's Cornish clotted vanilla ice cream | 125ml, 2 scoops | 135 | 8.9 | 5.7 | 12 | 1.7 | 0.1 |
| Kelly's Cornish strawberries & cream | 125ml, 2 scoops | 125 | 5.9 | 5.2 | 16 | 1.9 | Tr |
| Magnum classic | 120ml, 1 stick | 260 | 16 | 12 | 25 | 3.0 | 1.5 |
| Magnum gold | 120ml, 1 stick | 280 | 18 | 14 | 26 | 3.0 | 0.5 |
| Magnum white | 120ml, 1 stick | 270 | 16 | 12 | 26 | 3.5 | 0.3 |
| Mars ice cream bar | 51ml, 1 bar | 143 | 8.3 | * | 15 | 1.8 | * |
| Nestlé Fab | 59ml, 1 stick | 90 | 3.2 | 1.4 | 15 | 0.3 | 0.3 |
| Skinny Cow mint double choc ice cream bar | 100ml, 1 stick | 94 | 1.9 | 1.2 | 15 | 2.4 | 3.0 |
| Skinny Cow triple choc brownie | 100ml, 1 stick | 93 | 1.7 | 1.0 | 16 | 2.3 | 3.4 |
| Solero fruit ice, orange | 55ml, 1 stick | 65 | Tr | Tr | 15 | Tr | Tr |
| Strawberry Split | 73ml, 1 stick | 67 | 1.8 | 1.1 | 12 | 0.7 | 0.2 |
| Wall's Classics Cornish vanilla | 100ml, 2 scoops | 75 | 3.0 | 2.0 | 11 | 1.5 | 0.5 |
| Wall's Soft Scoop vanilla ice cream | 100ml, 2 scoops | 85 | 4.0 | 2.0 | 10 | 1.5 | 0.5 |

| Crisps & snacks | Av Portion | Calories | Fat, g | Saturated fat, g | Carbohydrate, g | Protein, g | Fibre, g |
|---|---|---|---|---|---|---|---|
| Burt's potato chips, sea salted | 50g | 271 | 14 | 1.5 | 23 | 2.6 | * |
| Doritos, cool original | 35g | 175 | 9.5 | 0.9 | 20 | 2.6 | 1.1 |
| Doritos, tangy cheese | 35g | 175 | 9.3 | 1.1 | 20 | 2.9 | 1.1 |
| Hula hoops | 34g | 175 | 9.7 | 0.9 | 21 | 1.1 | 0.6 |
| Hula hoops big hoops, chilli | 25g | 127 | 6.6 | 0.6 | 16 | 0.9 | 0.6 |
| Kallo breadsticks, original | 25g | 100 | 1.6 | 0.3 | 19 | 2.5 | 0.3 |
| Kallo Torinesi breadsticks, with parmesan | 25g | 103 | 2.1 | 0.8 | 18 | 3.3 | 0.3 |
| Kettle Chips, Cheddar & red onion | 40g | 187 | 10 | 1.2 | 21 | 3.0 | 2.5 |
| Kettle Chips, lightly salted | 40g | 192 | 10 | 1.2 | 22 | 2.5 | 2.0 |
| Kettle vegetable chips | 25g | 121 | 8.5 | 0.9 | 9.8 | 1.4 | 3.2 |
| Marmite rice cakes | 22g | 86 | 0.6 | 0.1 | 17 | 3.3 | 0.8 |
| McCoy's ridge cut crisps, flame-grilled steak | 50g | 259 | 15 | 1.4 | 27 | 3.5 | 2.0 |
| McCoy's ridge cut crisps, Mexican chilli | 50g | 257 | 15 | 1.4 | 27 | 3.5 | 2.3 |
| McCoy's ridge cut crisps, salt & malt vinegar | 50g | 258 | 15 | 1.4 | 27 | 3.4 | 2.0 |
| Mini Cheddars | 25g | 162 | 7.5 | 3.0 | 13 | 3.0 | 0.7 |
| New York Style bagel crisps | 50g | 232 | 11 | 4.5 | 30 | 3.6 | 3.6 |
| New York Style pitta crisps | 50g | 242 | 10 | 2.7 | 33 | 5.7 | 1.7 |
| Penn State pretzels, salted | 50g | 188 | 0.5 | Tr | 9.3 | 1.3 | 0.6 |
| Pringles, original | 25g | 131 | 8.4 | 1.8 | 13 | 1.0 | 0.7 |
| Pringles, salt & vinegar | 25g | 129 | 8.0 | 1.7 | 13 | 0.9 | 0.6 |
| Pringles, sour cream & onion | 25g | 129 | 8.2 | 1.8 | 13 | 1.0 | 0.6 |
| Quavers, cheese | 20g | 109 | 6.2 | 0.6 | 13 | 0.6 | 0.2 |
| Red Sky crisps, Anglesey sea salt | 40g | 185 | 8.7 | 0.7 | 24 | 2.7 | 2.0 |
| Red Sky crisps, English Cheddar & red onion | 40g | 183 | 8.4 | 0.7 | 24 | 2.8 | 2.0 |
| Red Sky crisps, sour cream & green herb | 40g | 188 | 9.4 | 1.0 | 23 | 2.7 | 1.9 |
| Ryvitas Minis, salt & vinegar | 30g | 94 | 0.8 | 0.1 | 19 | 2.0 | 3.6 |
| Snack-a-Jacks Jumbos, cheese | 10g (1 cake) | 38 | 0.3 | 0.1 | 8.1 | 0.9 | 0.2 |

| Crisps & snacks | Av Portion | Calories | Fat, g | Saturated fat, g | Carbohydrate, g | Protein, g | Fibre, g |
|---|---|---|---|---|---|---|---|
| Snack-a-Jacks, salt & vinegar | 22g | 89 | 1.6 | 0.1 | 9.1 | 0.9 | 0.2 |
| Tyrell's crisps, lightly salted | 40g | 197 | 10 | 0.9 | 24 | 3.1 | 1.0 |
| Tyrell's crisps, mature Cheddar & chives | 40g | 194 | 10 | 1.1 | 24 | 3.4 | 1.0 |
| Tyrell's crisps, sea salt & black pepper | 40g | 194 | 10 | 1.1 | 24 | 3.4 | 1.0 |
| Tyrell's crisps, sea salt & cider vinegar | 40g | 197 | 9.8 | 0.9 | 24 | 3.1 | 1.0 |
| Tyrell's popcorn, sweet & salty | 20g | 90 | 4.9 | 0.6 | 10 | 1.3 | 2.4 |
| Tyrell's vegetable crisps | 25g | 184 | 13 | 1.4 | 14 | 2.0 | 4.8 |
| Walkers Baked, cheese & onion | 25g | 99 | 2.1 | 0.3 | 18 | 1.6 | 1.4 |
| Walkers Baked, ready salted | 25g | 98 | 2.0 | 0.3 | 19 | 1.5 | 1.4 |
| Walkers Baked, salt & vinegar | 25g | 98 | 2.0 | 0.3 | 18 | 1.5 | 1.3 |
| Walkers crisps, cheese & onion | 34.5g | 184 | 11 | 0.9 | 17 | 2.4 | 1.4 |
| Walkers crisps, ready salted | 34.5g | 185 | 12 | 0.9 | 17 | 2.0 | 1.4 |
| Walkers crisps, salt & vinegar | 34.5g | 181 | 11 | 0.9 | 17 | 2.0 | 1.4 |
| Walkers crisps, steak & onion | 34.5g | 183 | 11 | 0.9 | 17 | 2.1 | 1.4 |
| Walkers Lights, sour cream & onion | 25g | 115 | 5.3 | 0.5 | 15 | 1.8 | 1.1 |
| Walkers Lights, cheese & onion | 25g | 115 | 5.3 | 0.5 | 15 | 1.8 | 1.1 |
| Walkers Lights, simply salted | 25g | 115 | 5.3 | 0.5 | 15 | 1.7 | 1.2 |
| Walkers Max, chargrilled steak | 50g | 262 | 16 | 2.1 | 26 | 3.6 | 1.5 |
| Walkers Max, cheese & onion | 50g | 264 | 17 | 2.1 | 26 | 3.4 | 1.5 |
| Walkers Max, cheeseburger | 50g | 266 | 16 | 2.1 | 26 | 3.3 | 1.5 |
| Walkers Sensations, balsamic vinegar & caramelised onion | 35g | 170 | 9.1 | 0.9 | 20 | 2.1 | 1.5 |
| Walkers Sensations, lime & coriander poppadoms | 35g | 168 | 8.0 | 0.8 | 22 | 2.6 | 1.6 |
| Walkers Sensations, Thai sweet chilli | 35g | 170 | 9.1 | 0.7 | 20 | 2.1 | 1.5 |
| Walkers Sunbites, sea salted | 25g | 120 | 5.4 | 0.6 | 15 | 1.8 | 1.7 |
| Walkers Sunbites, sour cream | 25g | 120 | 5.4 | 0.6 | 15 | 1.9 | 1.7 |

| Eating out & takeaways | Av Portion | Calories | Fat, g | Saturated fat, g | Carbohydrate, g | Protein, g | Fibre, g |
|---|---|---|---|---|---|---|---|
| **BURGER KING** | | | | | | | |
| Angus burger | | 580 | 31 | 9 | 41 | 31 | 2 |
| Chicken royale | | 608 | 32 | 4 | 51 | 25 | 3 |
| Fries | Regular | 291 | 12 | 4 | 39 | 4 | 5 |
| Hamburger | | 284 | 11 | 4 | 30 | 15 | 1 |
| Veggie bean burger | | 590 | 20 | 5 | 83 | 18 | 8 |
| Whopper | | 651 | 36 | 9 | 51 | 29 | 2 |
| **CAFFÉ NERO** | | | | | | | |
| Chicken Caesar wrap | Each | 434 | 23 | 5.0 | 36 | 21 | 1.3 |
| Chicken salad sandwich | Each | 272 | 4.2 | 0.6 | 38 | 19 | 3.0 |
| Falafel wrap | Each | 434 | 22 | 5.3 | 46 | 14 | 2.9 |
| Ham & free-range egg mayonnaise breakfast muffin | Each | 314 | 12 | 2.1 | 35 | 15 | 2.3 |
| Pesto chicken panini | Each | 385 | 13 | 2.5 | 41 | 25 | 2.4 |
| Tuna melt panini | Each | 389 | 14 | 7.2 | 42 | 23 | 2.3 |
| Vine tomato, mozzarella & basil panini | Each | 398 | 17 | 7.5 | 43 | 18 | 2.7 |
| **CHINESE** | | | | | | | |
| Beef chow mein | 350g | 476 | 21 | 4.5 | 51 | 23 | * |
| Chicken chow mein | 350g | 515 | 25 | 4.1 | 44 | 30 | 3.9 |
| Chicken satay | 200g | 382 | 21 | 6.0 | 6.0 | 43 | 4.4 |
| Crispy duck | 200g | 662 | 48 | 14 | 0.6 | 56 | 0 |
| Fried noodles | 230g | 352 | 26 | * | 26 | 4.4 | 1.2 |
| Plain noodles | 230g | 143 | 1.0 | 0.2 | 30 | 5.5 | 1.6 |
| Prawn crackers | 70g | 399 | 27 | 2.5 | 41 | 0.2 | 0.8 |
| Sweet & sour chicken | 400g | 776 | 40 | 5.2 | 79 | 30 | * |
| **FISH AND CHIPS** | | | | | | | |
| Chips, fried vegetable oil | 165g | 394 | 20 | 5.9 | 50 | 5.3 | 3.6 |
| Cod in batter | 180g | 445 | 28 | 7.4 | 21 | 29 | 0.9 |
| Haddock in batter | 220g | 510 | 31 | 8.1 | 22 | 38 | 0.9 |
| Plaice in batter | 200g | 514 | 34 | 9.0 | 24 | 30 | 1.0 |
| Rock salmon in batter | 125g | 369 | 27 | 6.6 | 13 | 18 | 0.5 |
| **INDIAN** | | | | | | | |
| Chicken curry | 400g | 580 | 39 | 12 | 10 | 47 | 8.0 |
| Chicken tikka masala | 400g | 628 | 42 | 15 | 10 | 52 | 6.4 |
| Naan bread | 160g | 456 | 12 | 1.6 | 80 | 13 | 3.2 |
| Pilau rice | 250g | 543 | 29 | * | 64 | 6.8 | 1.5 |
| Poppadums | 20g | 100 | 8.0 | 1.6 | 5.7 | 2.3 | 1.2 |
| Prawn curry | 350g | 410 | 30 | 4.9 | 7.7 | 29 | 7.0 |
| Samosa, meat | 70g | 190 | 12 | 3.1 | 13 | 8.0 | 1.7 |
| Samosa, vegetable | 70g | 152 | 7.0 | * | 21 | 3.6 | 1.8 |
| Vegetable curry | 200g | 210 | 15 | 3.0 | 15 | 5.0 | * |

| Eating out & takeaways | Av Portion | Calories | Fat, g | Saturated fat, g | Carbohydrate, g | Protein, g | Fibre, g |
|---|---|---|---|---|---|---|---|
| **JD WETHERSPOON** | | | | | | | |
| 8oz sirloin steak, chips, peas & tomato | | 987 | 60 | 19 | 69 | 57 | 11 |
| Breaded scampi, chips & peas | | 996 | 49 | 5.4 | 111 | 32 | 12 |
| Chicken Caesar salad | | 623 | 41 | 13 | 16 | 47 | 2.5 |
| Classic 6oz beefburger | | 1064 | 42 | 12 | 108 | 43 | 8.9 |
| Hand-battered fish, chips & peas | | 1182 | 66 | 13 | 97 | 52 | 11 |
| Roast of the day: beef | | 679 | 18 | 5.2 | 68 | 62 | 14 |
| Roast of the day: half roast chicken | | 1187 | 59 | 16 | 67 | 97 | 9.6 |
| Sausages & mash | | 715 | 31 | 11 | 69 | 39 | 12 |
| Steak & kidney pudding | | 1143 | 64 | 25 | 110 | 33 | 11 |
| **KFC** | | | | | | | |
| Fillet burger | | 449 | 16 | 2.8 | 7.7 | 21 | * |
| Flamin' wrap | | 337 | 16 | 3.8 | 30 | 18 | * |
| Fried chicken | 3 pieces | 735 | 43 | 9 | 23 | 63 | * |
| Fried chicken | 1 piece | 244 | 15 | 2.8 | 7.7 | 21 | * |
| Fries | Regular | 247 | 12 | 1.3 | 37 | 3.7 | * |
| Hot wings | 1 wing | 81 | 5.6 | 0.9 | 2.9 | 5.0 | * |
| Popcorn chicken | Regular | 283 | 17 | 1.6 | 15 | 18 | * |
| Zinger burger | | 476 | 19 | 3.1 | 48 | 28 | * |
| **MCDONALD'S** | | | | | | | |
| Big Mac | | 490 | 24 | 10 | 41 | 28 | 4 |
| Cheeseburger | | 295 | 12 | 6 | 31 | 16 | 2 |
| Chicken McNuggets | 6 pieces | 250 | 14 | 2 | 20 | 14 | 1 |
| Filet-o-Fish | | 350 | 16 | 3 | 36 | 15 | 2 |
| French fries | Medium | 330 | 16 | 2 | 42 | 3 | 4 |
| Hamburger | | 250 | 8.0 | 3 | 30 | 14 | 2 |
| Spicy vegetable wrap | | 445 | 16 | 3 | 59 | 10 | 10 |
| Sweet chilli crispy chicken wrap | | 460 | 18 | 3 | 53 | 20 | 3 |
| **PIZZA HUT** | | | | | | | |
| BBQ American, large pan | 1 slice | 310 | 12 | 4.0 | 35 | 16 | * |
| BBQ American, regular pan | 1 slice | 202 | 8.3 | 2.7 | 22 | 9.8 | * |
| Chicken supreme, large pan | 1 slice | 279 | 11 | 3.5 | 31 | 14 | * |
| Chicken supreme, regular pan | 1 slice | 184 | 7.6 | 2.4 | 20 | 8.9 | * |
| Hawaiian, large pan | 1 slice | 275 | 11 | 3.6 | 32 | 12 | * |
| Hawaiian, regular pan | 1 slice | 183 | 7.7 | 2.5 | 21 | 8.1 | * |
| Margherita, large pan | 1 slice | 282 | 13 | 4.6 | 31 | 11 | * |
| Margherita, large stuffed crust | 1 slice | 328 | 15 | 7.4 | 34 | 15 | * |
| Margherita, regular pan | 1 slice | 188 | 8.7 | 3.1 | 20 | 7.5 | * |
| Meat feast, large pan | 1 slice | 316 | 15 | 4.7 | 31 | 16 | * |
| Meat feast, regular pan | 1 slice | 190 | 8.5 | 2.4 | 20 | 8.8 | * |
| Veggie supreme, large pan | 1 slice | 262 | 11 | 3.5 | 32 | 9.9 | * |
| Veggie supreme, regular pan | 1 slice | 156 | 6.2 | 1.7 | 20 | 5.3 | * |

| Eating out & takeways | Av Portion | Calories | Fat, g | Saturated fat, g | Carbohydrate, g | Protein, g | Fibre, g |
|---|---|---|---|---|---|---|---|
| **STARBUCKS** | | | | | | | |
| Almond croissant | Each | 433 | 22 | 9.7 | 52 | 5.2 | 1.5 |
| Butter croissant | Each | 266 | 16 | 9.3 | 27 | 4.1 | 0.9 |
| Caffe latte, skimmed | Tall | 102 | 0.2 | 0.2 | 15 | 9.9 | 0 |
| Caffe Americano | Tall | 12 | 0 | 0 | 2.0 | 0.7 | 0 |
| Caffe latte, semi-skimmed | Tall | 148 | 5.6 | 3.6 | 14 | 9.7 | 0 |
| Caffe mocha, semi-skimmed, with whipped cream | Tall | 266 | 13 | 7.1 | 33 | 10 | 1.4 |
| Cappuccino, semi-skimmed | Tall | 91 | 3.4 | 2.2 | 9.0 | 6.0 | 0 |
| Cappuccino, skimmed | Tall | 64 | 0.1 | 0.1 | 9.5 | 6.1 | 0 |
| Cheese & Marmite panini | Each | 382 | 18 | 11 | 35 | 20 | 1.4 |
| Classic blueberry muffin | Each | 481 | 22 | 2.2 | 256 | 6.0 | 2.1 |
| Classic hot chocolate, semi-skimmed, with whipped cream | Tall | 261 | 13 | 7.1 | 32 | 10 | 1.4 |
| Frapuccino, coffee, semi-skimmed | Tall | 170 | 1.6 | 1.0 | 36 | 2.8 | 0.1 |
| Mozzarella & slow roast tomato panini | Each | 468 | 20 | 8.1 | 50 | 20 | 2.7 |
| Pain au chocolat | Each | 269 | 20 | 9.5 | 27 | 3.7 | 1.7 |
| Pain aux raisins | Each | 373 | 19 | 11 | 44 | 5.2 | 1.5 |
| Roasted chicken & tomato panini | Each | 347 | 8.0 | 0.9 | 51 | 21 | 3.1 |
| Skinny blueberry muffin | Each | 372 | 5.5 | 0.8 | 73 | 5.8 | 3.2 |

| Eggs | Av Portion | Calories | Fat, g | Saturated fat, g | Carbohydrate, g | Protein, g | Fibre, g |
|---|---|---|---|---|---|---|---|
| Duck eggs, raw | 75g (1 egg) | 122 | 9.0 | 2.2 | 0 | 11 | 0 |
| Egg white | 32g (1 egg) | 12 | 0 | 0 | 0 | 2.9 | 0 |
| Egg yolk | 18g (1 egg) | 61 | 5.0 | 1.6 | 0 | 2.9 | 0 |
| Eggs, boiled | 50g (1 egg) | 74 | 5.0 | 1.5 | 0 | 6.3 | 0 |
| Eggs, fried | 60g (1 egg) | 107 | 8.0 | 2.4 | 0 | 8.2 | 0 |
| Eggs, poached | 50g (1 egg) | 74 | 5.0 | 1.5 | 0 | 6.3 | 0 |
| Eggs, raw, size 2 | 61g (1 egg) | 87 | 7.0 | 1.8 | 0 | 7.6 | 0 |
| Eggs, raw, size 3 | 57g (1 egg) | 82 | 6.0 | 1.7 | 0 | 7.1 | 0 |
| Eggs, scrambled with milk | 120g (2 eggs) | 308 | 28 | 14 | 0.8 | 13 | 0 |
| Omelette, plain | 120g (2 eggs) | 234 | 20 | 8.7 | 0 | 13 | 0 |
| Quail eggs | 10g (1 egg) | 15 | 1.0 | 0.3 | 0 | 1.3 | 0 |

| Fats, oils & spreads | Av Portion | Calories | Fat, g | Saturated fat, g | Carbohydrate, g | Protein, g | Fibre, g |
|---|---|---|---|---|---|---|---|
| **FATS** | | | | | | | |
| Anchor spreadable | 10g (2 tsp) | 72 | 8.0 | 3.1 | 0.1 | 0.1 | 0 |
| Benecol spread | 10g (2 tsp) | 58 | 6.3 | 1.5 | 0.1 | Tr | 0 |
| Bertolli spread | 10g (2 tsp) | 54 | 5.9 | 1.4 | 0.1 | Tr | 0 |
| Butter | 10g (2 tsp) | 74 | 8.0 | 5.2 | 0.1 | 0.1 | 0 |
| Clover spread | 10g (2 tsp) | 67 | 7.5 | 2.7 | 0.1 | 0.1 | 0 |
| Flora light spread | 10g (2 tsp) | 35 | 3.8 | 0.9 | 0.3 | Tr | 0 |
| Flora original spread | 10g (2 tsp) | 53 | 5.9 | 1.2 | Tr | Tr | 0 |
| Flora Pro-activ spread | 10g (2 tsp) | 32 | 3.5 | 0.9 | 0.3 | Tr | 0 |
| Ghee | 10g (2 tsp) | 90 | 10 | 6.6 | 0 | 0 | 0 |
| I Can't Believe It's Not Butter | 10g (2 tsp) | 62 | 7.0 | 2.4 | 0.1 | 0.1 | 0 |
| Lard | 15g (1 tbsp) | 134 | 15 | 6.0 | 0 | 0 | 0 |
| Lurpak spreadable | 10g (2 tsp) | 73 | 8.0 | 4.0 | 0.1 | 0.1 | 0 |
| Margarine, polyunsaturated | 10g (2 tsp) | 75 | 8.0 | 1.7 | 0 | 0 | 0 |
| Pure sunflower spread | 10g (2 tsp) | 60 | 6.7 | 1.5 | 0 | 0 | 0 |
| Suet | 15g (1 tbsp) | 124 | 13 | 7.5 | 1.8 | 0 | 0 |
| **OILS** | | | | | | | |
| Coconut oil | 11g (1 tbsp) | 99 | 11 | 9.5 | 0 | 0 | 0 |
| Corn oil | 11g (1 tbsp) | 99 | 11 | 1.6 | 0 | 0 | 0 |
| Frylight sunflower oil spray | 0.7g (4 sprays) | 4 | 0.4 | Tr | Tr | Tr | 0 |
| Olive oil | 11g (1 tbsp) | 99 | 11 | 2.2 | 0 | 0 | 0 |
| Sesame oil | 11g (1 tbsp) | 99 | 11 | 1.6 | 0 | 0 | 0 |
| Soya oil | 11g (1 tbsp) | 99 | 11 | 1.7 | 0 | 0 | 0 |
| Sunflower oil | 11g (1 tbsp) | 99 | 11 | 1.3 | 0 | 0 | 0 |
| Vegetable oil, blended | 11g (1 tbsp) | 99 | 11 | 1.3 | 0 | 0 | 0 |
| **SAVOURY SPREADS** | | | | | | | |
| Cheese spread | 15g (1 tbsp) | 40 | 3.0 | 2.4 | 0.7 | 1.7 | 0 |
| Dairylea cheese spread | 25g (1 tbsp) | 59 | 4.9 | 3.2 | 1.1 | 2.7 | 0 |
| Dairylea cheese triangles | 17.5g (1 triangle) | 43 | 3.3 | 2.2 | 1.1 | 2.0 | 0 |
| Dairylea light cheese triangles | 17.5g (1 triangle) | 26 | 1.2 | 0.8 | 1.0 | 2.6 | 0 |
| Fish paste | 10g (2 tsp) | 17 | 1.0 | * | 0.4 | 1.5 | 0 |
| The Laughing Cow cheese portions | 17.5g (1 portion) | 42 | 3.3 | 2.3 | 1.0 | 1.9 | 0 |
| Liver pâté | 40g (1 tbsp) | 139 | 13 | 3.8 | 0.3 | 5.0 | 0 |
| Marmite | 4g (1 tsp) | 9 | 0 | 0 | 0.8 | 1.5 | 0.1 |
| **SWEET SPREADS** | | | | | | | |
| Cadbury's milk chocolate spread | 15g (1 tbsp) | 86 | 5.6 | * | 8.1 | 0.6 | * |
| Nutella hazelnut and chocolate spread | 15g (1 tbsp) | 80 | 4.7 | 1.5 | 8.5 | 1.0 | 0.5 |
| Fruit spread | 15g (1 tbsp) | 18 | 0 | 0 | 4.7 | 0.1 | * |
| Honey | 20g (1 tbsp) | 58 | 0 | 0 | 15 | 0.1 | 0 |
| Jam, fruit with seeds | 15g (1 tbsp) | 39 | 0 | 0 | 10 | 0.1 | * |
| Jam, stone fruit | 15g (1 tbsp) | 39 | 0 | 0 | 10 | 0.1 | * |
| Lemon curd | 15g (1 tbsp) | 42 | 1.0 | 0.2 | 9.4 | 0.1 | 0 |
| Marmalade | 15g (1 tbsp) | 39 | 0 | 0 | 10 | 0 | 0 |
| Reduced sugar jam, Weight Watcher's, apricot | 15g (1 tbsp) | 24 | 0 | 0 | 5.8 | 0 | 0.2 |

| Fish & seafood | Av Portion | Calories | Fat, g | Saturated fat, g | Carbohydrate, g | Protein, g | Fibre, g |
|---|---|---|---|---|---|---|---|
| **FISH** | | | | | | | |
| Anchovies, canned in oil, drained | 10g (3) | 19 | 1.0 | 0.2 | 0 | 2.5 | 0 |
| Bass, sea | 120g | 120 | 3.0 | 0.5 | 0 | 23 | 0 |
| Bream, sea | 120g | 115 | 3.0 | * | 0 | 21 | 0 |
| Cod, baked | 120g | 115 | 1.0 | 0.4 | 0 | 26 | 0 |
| Cod, poached | 120g | 113 | 2.0 | 0.7 | 0 | 25 | 0 |
| Cod, smoked, poached | 120g | 121 | 1.0 | 0.2 | 0 | 26 | 0 |
| Coley, steamed | 120g | 126 | 2.0 | 0.2 | 0 | 28 | 0 |
| Dover sole | 140g | 125 | 3.0 | * | 0 | 25 | 0 |
| Haddock, grilled | 120g | 125 | 1.0 | 0.2 | 0 | 29 | 0 |
| Haddock, poached | 120g | 136 | 5.0 | 3.1 | 1.3 | 21 | 0 |
| Haddock, smoked, poached | 150g | 201 | 9.0 | 5.6 | 1.7 | 28 | 0 |
| Halibut, grilled | 145g | 175 | 3.0 | 0.6 | 0 | 37 | 0 |
| Halibut, poached | 110g | 169 | 6.0 | 3.0 | 1.2 | 27 | 0 |
| Herring, grilled | 110g | 199 | 12 | 3.1 | 0 | 22 | 0 |
| Kipper, baked | 130g | 267 | 15 | 2.3 | 0 | 33 | 0 |
| Kipper, grilled | 130g | 332 | 25 | 4.0 | 0 | 26 | 0 |
| Lemon sole, grilled | 110g | 107 | 2.0 | 0.2 | 0 | 22 | 0 |
| Mackerel, canned in brine, drained | 200g | 474 | 36 | 8.0 | 0 | 38 | 0 |
| Mackerel, canned in tomato sauce | 125g | 258 | 19 | 4.1 | 1.7 | 21 | 0 |
| Mackerel, grilled | 150g | 359 | 26 | 5.3 | 0 | 38 | 0 |
| Mackerel, smoked | 150g | 531 | 46 | 9.5 | 0 | 28 | 0 |
| Monkfish, grilled | 120g | 115 | 1.0 | 0.1 | 0 | 27 | 0 |
| Pilchards, canned in tomato sauce | 215g (1 tin) | 310 | 17 | 3.7 | 2.4 | 26 | 0 |
| Plaice, grilled | 130g | 125 | 2.0 | 0.4 | 0 | 26 | 0 |
| Pollack, Alaskan | 140g | 101 | 1.0 | 0.1 | 0 | 23 | 0 |
| Red snapper, fried | 120g | 151 | 4.0 | 0.8 | 0 | 29 | 0 |
| Salmon, grilled | 115g | 247 | 15 | 2.9 | 0 | 28 | 0 |
| Salmon, canned in brined, drained | 100g (1 tin) | 153 | 7.0 | 1.3 | 0 | 24 | 0 |
| Salmon, smoked | 110g | 156 | 5.0 | 0.9 | 0 | 28 | 0 |
| Sardines, canned in brine, drained | 100g (1 tin) | 172 | 10 | * | 0 | 22 | 0 |
| Sardines, canned in oil, drained | 100g (1 tin) | 220 | 14 | 2.9 | 0 | 23 | 0 |
| Sardines, canned in tomato sauce | 100g (1 tin) | 162 | 10 | 2.8 | 1.4 | 17 | 0 |
| Sardines, grilled | 40g | 78 | 4.0 | 1.2 | 0 | 10 | 0 |
| Swordfish, grilled | 125g | 174 | 6.0 | 1.5 | 0 | 29 | 0 |
| Trout, rainbow, grilled | 155g | 209 | 8.0 | 1.7 | 0 | 33 | 0 |
| Tuna | 120g | 163 | 6.0 | 1.4 | 0 | 28 | 0 |
| Tuna, canned in brine, drained | 100g (1 tin) | 99 | 1.0 | 0.2 | 0 | 24 | 0 |
| Tuna, canned in oil, drained | 100g (1 tin) | 189 | 9.0 | 1.5 | 0 | 27 | 0 |

*No information available  Tr trace quantities<0.1g

| Fish & seafood | Av Portion | Calories | Fat, g | Saturated fat, g | Carbohydrate, g | Protein, g | Fibre, g |
|---|---|---|---|---|---|---|---|
| **SEAFOOD** | | | | | | | |
| Clams, canned in brine, drained | 50g | 39 | 0.5 | 0.1 | 0.9 | 8.0 | 0 |
| Cockles, boiled | 25g | 13 | 0.5 | 0.1 | 0 | 3.0 | 0 |
| Crab, boiled | 85g | 109 | 5.0 | 0.6 | 0 | 17 | 0 |
| Lobster, boiled, weighed with shell | 250g | 93 | 2.0 | 0.3 | 0 | 20 | 0 |
| Mussels, boiled, weighed with shells | 90g | 25 | 1.0 | 0.1 | 0.8 | 4.1 | 0 |
| Oysters, weighed with shells | 500g | 45 | 1.0 | Tr | 2.0 | 7.5 | 0 |
| Prawns, boiled | 60g | 59 | 1.0 | 0.1 | 0 | 9.5 | 0 |
| Scallops, steamed | 70g | 83 | 1.0 | 0.3 | 2.4 | 16 | 0 |
| Scampi, in breadcrumbs, fried | 170g | 403 | 23 | 2.7 | 25 | 16 | * |
| Shrimps, boiled | 50g | 59 | 1.0 | 0.2 | 0 | 12 | 0 |
| Squid | 140g | 113 | 2.0 | 0.6 | 1.7 | 22 | 0 |
| Whelks | 30g | 27 | 0.5 | 0.1 | 0 | 5.9 | 0 |
| Winkles | 30g | 22 | 0.5 | 0.1 | 0 | 4.6 | 0 |

| Fish products | Av Portion | Calories | Fat, g | Saturated fat, g | Carbohydrate, g | Protein, g | Fibre, g |
|---|---|---|---|---|---|---|---|
| Bird's Eye cod fish cakes in crunch crumbs | 100g (2 cakes) | 187 | 8.5 | 1.1 | 16 | 12 | 1.0 |
| Bird's Eye cod fish fingers | 84g (3 fingers) | 185 | 7.6 | 0.8 | 18 | 11 | 0.8 |
| Bird's Eye fish fillets in breadcrumbs | 100g (1 fillet) | 218 | 8.2 | 1.1 | 24 | 12 | 1.2 |
| Bird's Eye omega 3 fish fingers | 84g (3 fingers) | 185 | 7.8 | 0.9 | 18 | 10 | 0.8 |
| Bird's Eye salmon fish fingers | 84g (3 fingers) | 190 | 8.0 | 0.9 | 18 | 11 | 0.8 |
| Bird's Eye Simply fish fillets in batter | 100g (1 fillet) | 235 | 13 | 1.7 | 19 | 11 | 0.7 |
| Jamie Oliver crispy salmon and pollock fish cakes | 100g ( 2 cakes) | 190 | 8.6 | 0.9 | 17 | 9.9 | 1.7 |
| Young's breaded haddock fillets | 125g (1 fillet) | 234 | 8.7 | 1.0 | 22 | 17 | 1.5 |
| Young's fish cakes | 106g (2 cakes) | 168 | 6.6 | 2.0 | 19 | 9.0 | 1.4 |
| Young's haddock fish fingers | 87g (3 fingers) | 160 | 8.0 | 0.9 | 11 | 12 | 1.2 |
| Young's omega 3 fish fingers | 100g (4 fingers) | 216 | 11 | 1.2 | 17 | 13 | 0.8 |
| Young's Chip Shop large fish fillets | 20g (1 fillet) | 262 | 15 | 2.8 | 18 | 13 | 1.1 |
| Young's cod steaks in butter sauce | 140g (1 steak) | 107 | 3.2 | 2.2 | 5.8 | 14 | 0.6 |
| Young's cod steaks in parsley sauce | 140g (1 steak) | 101 | 2.6 | 1.7 | 5.9 | 13 | 0.6 |
| Bird's Eye baked to perfection haddock fillets | 280g | 175 | 7.8 | 5.0 | 2.5 | 24 | 0.2 |
| Bird's Eye baked to perfection wild pink salmon fillets | 280g | 200 | 12 | 6.5 | 0.6 | 23 | tr |
| Young's fish and chips | 300g | 489 | 22 | 2.1 | 53 | 20 | 4.2 |
| Young's original ocean pie | 400g | 440 | 16 | 7.7 | 47 | 24 | 4.8 |

| Fruit | Av Portion | Calories | Fat, g | Saturated fat, g | Carbohydrate, g | Protein, g | Fibre, g |
|---|---|---|---|---|---|---|---|
| Apples, cooking, peeled | 130g (one) | 46 | Tr | 0 | 12 | 0.4 | 2.1 |
| Apples, eating | 100g (one) | 47 | Tr | 0 | 12 | 0.4 | 1.8 |
| Apricots, canned in juice | 80g | 27 | Tr | 0 | 6.7 | 0.4 | 0.7 |
| Apricots, canned in syrup | 80g | 50 | Tr | 0 | 13 | 0.3 | 0.7 |
| Apricots, fresh | 40g (one) | 12 | Tr | 0 | 2.9 | 0.4 | 0.7 |
| Apricots, dried, ready-to-eat | 40g (3) | 63 | Tr | 0 | 15 | 1.6 | 2.5 |
| Avocado | 145g (one) | 276 | 28 | 5.9 | 2.8 | 2.8 | 4.9 |
| Bananas | 100g (one) | 95 | 0.3 | 0 | 23 | 1.2 | 1.1 |
| Blackberries | 80g | 20 | Tr | 0 | 4.1 | 0.7 | 2.5 |
| Blackcurrants | 80g | 22 | Tr | 0 | 5.3 | 0.7 | 2.9 |
| Cherries, canned in syrup | 80g | 57 | Tr | 0 | 15 | 0.4 | 0.5 |
| Cherries, glacé | 25g (1 tbsp) | 63 | Tr | 0 | 17 | 0.1 | 0.2 |
| Cherries, fresh | 80g | 38 | Tr | 0 | 9.2 | 0.7 | 0.7 |
| Clementines | 60g (one) | 22 | Tr | 0 | 5.2 | 0.5 | 0.7 |
| Cranberries | 80g | 12 | Tr | 0 | 2.7 | 0.3 | 2.4 |
| Dates, dried | 25g (1 tbsp) | 68 | Tr | 0 | 17 | 0.8 | 1.0 |
| Dates, fresh | 25g (3) | 31 | Tr | 0 | 7.8 | 0.4 | 0.4 |
| Dried mixed fruit | 25g (1 handful) | 67 | Tr | 0 | 17 | 0.6 | 0.6 |
| Figs, fresh | 55g (one) | 24 | Tr | 0 | 5.2 | 0.7 | 0.9 |
| Figs, dried | 25g (3) | 52 | Tr | 0 | 12 | 0.8 | 1.7 |
| Fruit cocktail, canned in juice | 80g | 23 | Tr | 0 | 5.8 | 0.3 | 0.8 |
| Gooseberries | 80g | 32 | Tr | 0 | 7.4 | 0.6 | 1.9 |
| Grapefruit, canned in juice | 80g | 24 | Tr | 0 | 5.8 | 0.5 | 0.3 |
| Grapefruit, fresh | 80g (half) | 24 | Tr | 0 | 5.4 | 0.6 | 1.0 |
| Grapes | 80g | 48 | Tr | 0 | 12 | 0.3 | 0.6 |
| Guava, canned in syrup | 80g | 48 | Tr | 0 | 13 | 0.3 | 2.4 |
| Guava | 150g (one) | 39 | 0.8 | Tr | 7.5 | 1.2 | 5.6 |
| Kiwi fruit | 60g (one) | 29 | Tr | 0 | 6.4 | 0.7 | 1.1 |
| Lemon juice | 10g (half) | 1 | 0 | 0 | 0.2 | 0 | 0 |
| Lime juice | 10g (half) | 1 | 0 | 0 | 0.2 | 0 | 0 |
| Lychees, canned in syrup | 80g | 54 | Tr | 0 | 14 | 0.3 | 0.4 |
| Lychees, fresh | 15g (one) | 9 | Tr | 0 | 2.1 | 0.1 | 0.1 |
| Mandarin oranges, canned in juice | 80g | 26 | Tr | 0 | 6.2 | 0.6 | 0.2 |
| Mandarin oranges, canned in syrup | 80g | 42 | Tr | 0 | 11 | 0.4 | 0.2 |
| Mangoes | 150g (one) | 86 | Tr | 0 | 21 | 1.0 | 3.9 |

| Fruit | Av Portion | Calories | Fat, g | Saturated fat, g | Carbohydrate, g | Protein, g | Fibre, g |
|---|---|---|---|---|---|---|---|
| Melon, cantaloupe | 150g (1 slice) | 29 | Tr | 0 | 6.3 | 0.9 | 1.5 |
| Melon, galia | 150g (1 slice) | 36 | Tr | 0 | 8.4 | 0.8 | 0.6 |
| Melon, honeydew | 150g (1 slice) | 42 | Tr | 0 | 9.9 | 0.9 | 0.9 |
| Melon, watermelon | 200g (1 slice) | 62 | 0.3 | Tr | 14 | 1.0 | 0.2 |
| Nectarines | 150g (one) | 60 | Tr | 0 | 14 | 2.1 | 1.8 |
| Olives, in brine | 25g (1 handful) | 26 | 3.0 | 0.4 | 0 | 0.2 | 0.7 |
| Oranges | 160g (one) | 59 | Tr | 0 | 14 | 1.8 | 2.7 |
| Passion fruit | 15g (one) | 5 | Tr | 0 | 0.9 | 0.4 | 0.5 |
| Papaya | 140g (one) | 50 | Tr | 0 | 12 | 0.7 | 3.1 |
| Peaches | 110g (one) | 36 | tr | 0 | 8.4 | 1.1 | 1.6 |
| Peaches, canned in juice | 80g | 31 | tr | 0 | 7.8 | 0.5 | 0.6 |
| Peaches, canned in syrup | 80g | 44 | Tr | 0 | 11 | 0.4 | 0.7 |
| Pears | 160g (one) | 64 | Tr | 0 | 16 | 0.5 | 3.5 |
| Pears, canned in juice | 80g | 26 | Tr | 0 | 6.8 | 0.2 | 1.1 |
| Pears, canned in syrup | 80g | 40 | Tr | 0 | 11 | 0.2 | 0.9 |
| Pineapple, canned in juice | 80g | 38 | Tr | 0 | 9.8 | 0.2 | 0.4 |
| Pineapple, canned in syrup | 80g | 51 | Tr | 0 | 13 | 0.4 | 0.6 |
| Pineapple | 80g (2 rings) | 33 | Tr | 0 | 8.1 | 0.3 | 1.0 |
| Plums | 55g (one) | 20 | Tr | 0 | 4.8 | 0.3 | 0.9 |
| Plums, canned in syrup | 80g | 47 | Tr | 0 | 12 | 0.2 | 0.6 |
| Pomegranate | 100g (one) | 51 | Tr | 0 | 12 | 1.3 | 3.4 |
| Prunes, canned in juice | 80g | 64 | Tr | 0 | 16 | 0.6 | 2.0 |
| Prunes, canned in syrup | 80g | 72 | Tr | 0 | 18 | 0.4 | 2.2 |
| Prunes, ready-to-eat | 40g (8) | 56 | Tr | 0 | 14 | 1.0 | 2.3 |
| Raisins | 25g (1 handful) | 68 | Tr | 0 | 17 | 0.5 | 0.5 |
| Raspberries, canned in syrup | 80g | 70 | Tr | 0 | 18 | 0.5 | 1.2 |
| Raspberries | 80g | 20 | Tr | 0 | 3.7 | 1.1 | 2.0 |
| Redcurrants | 80g | 17 | Tr | 0 | 3.5 | 0.9 | 2.7 |
| Rhubarb, canned in syrup | 80g | 25 | Tr | 0 | 6.1 | 0.4 | 0.6 |
| Rhubarb | 80g | 6 | Tr | 0 | 0.6 | 0.7 | 1.1 |
| Satsumas | 60g (one) | 22 | Tr | 0 | 5.1 | 0.5 | 0.8 |
| Strawberries, canned in syrup | 80g | 52 | Tr | 0 | 14 | 0.4 | 0.6 |
| Strawberries | 80g | 22 | Tr | 0 | 4.8 | 0.6 | 0.9 |
| Sultanas | 25g (1 handful) | 69 | Tr | 0 | 17 | 0.7 | 0.5 |
| Tangerines | 60g (one) | 21 | Tr | 0 | 4.8 | 0.5 | 0.8 |

| Meat | Av Portion | Calories | Fat, g | Saturated fat, g | Carbohydrate, g | Protein, g | Fibre, g |
|---|---|---|---|---|---|---|---|
| **BACON** | | | | | | | |
| Back rashers, grilled | 15g (1 rasher) | 43 | 3.0 | 1.2 | 0 | 3.5 | 0 |
| Collar joint, boiled | 85g | 276 | 23 | 9.0 | 0 | 17 | 0 |
| Gammon joint, trimmed, boiled | 85g | 142 | 5.0 | 1.8 | 0 | 25 | 0 |
| Loin steak, grilled | 100g | 191 | 10 | 3.5 | 0 | 26 | 0 |
| Streaky rashers, grilled | 20g (1 rasher) | 67 | 5.0 | 2.0 | 0 | 4.8 | 0 |
| **BEEF** | | | | | | | |
| Beefburgers, fried | 50g | 165 | 12 | 5.3 | 0.1 | 14 | 0 |
| Beefburgers, grilled | 50g | 163 | 12 | 5.4 | 0.1 | 13 | 0 |
| Braising steak | 140g | 304 | 16 | 6.7 | 0 | 41 | 0 |
| Fillet steak, fried | 150g | 288 | 13 | 5.9 | 0 | 42 | 0 |
| Fillet steak, fried, trimmed | 150g | 276 | 12 | 5.1 | 0 | 42 | 0 |
| Fillet steak, grilled | 150g | 300 | 14 | 6.6 | 0 | 43 | 0 |
| Fillet steak, grilled, trimmed | 150g | 282 | 12 | 5.4 | 0 | 44 | 0 |
| Mince | 140g | 286 | 20 | 8.7 | 0 | 27 | 0 |
| Mince, lean | 140g | 244 | 13 | 5.9 | 0 | 31 | 0 |
| Rump steak, grilled | 150g | 306 | 14 | 7.8 | 0 | 44 | 0 |
| Sausages, fried | 45g | 126 | 9.0 | 3.4 | 5.6 | 6.1 | 0 |
| Sausages, grilled | 45g | 125 | 9.0 | 3.6 | 5.9 | 6.0 | 0 |
| Sirloin steak, fried, trimmed | 175g | 331 | 14 | 6.0 | 0 | 50 | 0 |
| Sirloin steak, fried | 175g | 408 | 25 | 11 | 0 | 47 | 0 |
| Sirloin steak, grilled | 175g | 373 | 22 | 9.8 | 0 | 43 | 0 |
| Sirloin steak, grilled, trimmed | 175g | 308 | 13 | 6.0 | 0 | 47 | 0 |
| Stewing steak, lean | 140g | 259 | 9.0 | 3.2 | 0 | 45 | 0 |
| Topside, roasted | 90g | 200 | 10 | 4.3 | 0 | 27 | 0 |
| Topside, roasted, trimmed | 90g | 158 | 5.0 | 1.9 | 0 | 29 | 0 |
| **BEEF DISHES** | | | | | | | |
| Beef bourguignon | 260g | 317 | 16 | 5.4 | 6.5 | 36 | 1.0 |
| Beef casserole | 300g | 408 | 20 | 8.2 | 14 | 45 | * |
| Beef curry | 350g | 480 | 23 | 11 | 22 | 47 | 4.2 |
| Chilli con carne | 220g | 211 | 9.0 | 4.2 | 16 | 17 | 3.1 |
| Shepherd's pie | 310g | 347 | 18 | 6.8 | 29 | 19 | 2.2 |
| Steak & kidney pie | 160g | 517 | 34 | 13 | 41 | 15 | 1.4 |
| **CHICKEN** | | | | | | | |
| Breast, grilled, skinned | 130g | 191 | 4.0 | 1.2 | 0 | 39 | 0 |
| Breast, grilled, with skin | 130g | 225 | 8.0 | 1.2 | 0 | 38 | 0 |
| Chicken curry | 350g | 522 | 31 | 14 | 19 | 42 | 4.5 |
| Chicken fricassée | 200g | 214 | 12 | 4.8 | 5.2 | 21 | 1.0 |
| Chicken goujons | 90g | 249 | 13 | 3.6 | 18 | 18 | 0.6 |
| Chicken Kiev | 170g | 456 | 29 | 12 | 19 | 32 | 1.0 |
| Chicken korma | 350g | 455 | 20 | 6.0 | 16 | 53 | 1.4 |
| Chicken pie | 130g | 374 | 23 | 9.1 | 32 | 12 | 1.0 |

| Meat | Av Portion | Calories | Fat, g | Saturated fat, g | Carbohydrate, g | Protein, g | Fibre, g |
|---|---|---|---|---|---|---|---|
| Chicken roll | 12g | 16 | 1.0 | 0.2 | 0.6 | 2.1 | 0 |
| Chicken slices | 40g | 46g | 1.0 | 0.2 | 0.8 | 9.3 | 0 |
| Coronation chicken | 200g | 728 | 63 | 11 | 6.4 | 33 | * |
| Drumsticks, roasted | 90g | 104 | 5.0 | 1.4 | 0 | 15 | 0 |
| Drumsticks, roasted, skinned | 47g | 71 | 2.0 | 0.7 | 0 | 13 | 0 |
| Leg quarter, casseroled | 146g | 317 | 20 | 5.5 | 0 | 33 | 0 |
| Leg quarter, casseroled, skinned | 146g | 257 | 12 | 3.4 | 0 | 37 | 0 |
| Leg quarter, roasted | 146g | 345 | 25 | 6.7 | 0 | 31 | 0 |
| Leg quarter, roasted, skinned | 146g | 134 | 5.0 | 1.5 | 0 | 23 | 0 |
| Thighs, casseroled | 45g | 105 | 7.0 | 2.0 | 0 | 10 | 0 |
| Thighs, casseroled, skinned | 45g | 81 | 4.0 | 1.1 | 0 | 12 | 0 |
| Whole, roasted | 100g | 218 | 13 | 3.4 | 0 | 26 | 0 |
| Wing quarter, casseroled | 150g | 315 | 19 | 5.3 | 0 | 37 | 0 |
| Wing quarter, casseroled, skinned | 150g | 246 | 9.0 | 2.6 | 0 | 40 | 0 |
| **GAME** | | | | | | | |
| Duck, roasted | 185g | 783 | 70 | 21 | 0 | 37 | 0 |
| Duck, roasted, skinned | 185g | 361 | 19 | 6.1 | 0 | 47 | 0 |
| Goose, roasted | 185g | 557 | 39 | 12 | 0 | 51 | 0 |
| Goose, roasted, skinned | 185g | 590 | 41 | * | 0 | 54 | 0 |
| Pheasant, roasted, skinned | 160g | 352 | 19 | 6.6 | 0 | 45 | 0 |
| Pigeon, roasted, skinned | 115g | 215 | 9.0 | * | 0 | 33 | 0 |
| Rabbit, stewed, skinned | 160g | 182 | 5.0 | 2.7 | 0 | 34 | 0 |
| Venison, roasted | 120g | 198 | 3.0 | * | 0 | 43 | 0 |
| **HAM** | | | | | | | |
| Parma | 45g | 100 | 6.0 | 1.9 | 0 | 12 | 0 |
| Premium | 23g | 30 | 1.0 | 0.4 | 0.1 | 4.9 | 0 |
| **LAMB** | | | | | | | |
| Neck cutlets, grilled, trimmed | 90g | 103 | 6.0 | 2.8 | 0 | 12 | 0 |
| Neck cutlets, grilled | 90g | 233 | 19 | 9.4 | 0 | 16 | 0 |
| Neck fillet, grilled, trimmed | 90g | 256 | 17 | 7.8 | 0 | 25 | 0 |
| Neck fillet, grilled | 90g | 272 | 20 | 9.3 | 0 | 23 | 0 |
| Chump chops, fried, trimmed | 70g | 149 | 8.0 | 3.5 | 0 | 20 | 0 |
| Chump chops, fried | 70g | 216 | 16 | 7.6 | 0 | 17 | 0 |
| Leg chops, grilled | 70g | 155 | 8.0 | 3.5 | 0 | 20 | 0 |
| Leg joint, roasted, trimmed | 90g | 189 | 9.0 | 3.1 | 0 | 28 | 0 |
| Leg joint, roasted | 90g | 212 | 12 | 4.2 | 0 | 27 | 0 |
| Leg steaks, grilled trimmed | 90g | 178 | 8.0 | 3.2 | 0 | 26 | 0 |
| Leg steaks, grilled | 90g | 208 | 12 | 5.0 | 0 | 25 | 0 |
| Loin chops, grilled, trimmed | 120g | 156 | 8.0 | 3.6 | 0 | 21 | 0 |
| Loin chops, grilled | 120g | 296 | 21 | 10 | 0 | 26 | 0 |
| Loin chops, roasted, trimmed | 70g | 180 | 9.0 | 4.3 | 0 | 24 | 0 |

| Meat | Av Portion | Calories | Fat, g | Saturated fat, g | Carbohydrate, g | Protein, g | Fibre, g |
|---|---|---|---|---|---|---|---|
| Loin chops, roasted | 120g | 379 | 25 | 14 | 0 | 27 | 0 |
| Loin joint, roasted, trimmed | 90g | 188 | 10 | 4.4 | 0 | 25 | 0 |
| Loin joint, roasted | 90g | 273 | 20 | 9.5 | 0 | 22 | 0 |
| Shoulder joint, roasted, trimmed | 90g | 212 | 12 | 5.6 | 0 | 26 | 0 |
| Shoulder joint, roasted | 90g | 254 | 18 | 8.4 | 0 | 23 | 0 |
| Mince | 100g | 208 | 12 | 5.8 | 0 | 24 | 0 |
| Rack of lamb, roasted, trimmed | 90g | 203 | 12 | 5.6 | 0 | 24 | 0 |
| Rack of lamb, roasted | 90g | 327 | 27 | 13 | 0 | 21 | 0 |
| **OFFAL** | | | | | | | |
| Kidneys, lambs, fried | 75g | 141 | 8.0 | * | 0 | 18 | 0 |
| Kidneys, pigs, stewed | 75g | 115 | 5.0 | 1.5 | 0 | 18 | 0 |
| Liver, calves, fried | 90g | 158 | 9.0 | * | 0 | 20 | 0 |
| Livers, chicken, fried | 90g | 152 | 8.0 | * | 0 | 20 | 0 |
| Liver, lambs, fried | 90g | 213 | 12 | * | 0 | 27 | 0 |
| **PORK** | | | | | | | |
| Belly joint, roasted | 110g | 322 | 24 | 8.1 | 0 | 28 | 0 |
| Fillet slices, grilled | 120g | 214 | 6.0 | 2.3 | 0 | 40 | 0 |
| Leg joint, roasted | 90g | 194 | 9.0 | 3.2 | 0 | 28 | 0 |
| Leg joint, roasted, trimmed | 90g | 164 | 5.0 | 1.7 | 0 | 30 | 0 |
| Loin chops, grilled | 120g | 308 | 19 | 6.7 | 0 | 35 | 0 |
| Loin chops, grilled, trimmed | 120g | 221 | 8.0 | 2.6 | 0 | 38 | 0 |
| Loin chops, roasted | 75g | 226 | 14 | 5.3 | 0 | 24 | 0 |
| Loin joint, roasted | 90g | 228 | 15 | 5.3 | 0 | 27 | 0 |
| Loin steaks, fried | 20g | 331 | 22 | 7.2 | 0 | 33 | 0 |
| Mince | 90g | 172 | 9.0 | 3.5 | 0 | 22 | 0 |
| Sausages, fried | 45g (1 sausage) | 139 | 11 | 3.8 | 4.5 | 6.3 | 0.3 |
| Sausages, grilled | 45g (1 sausage) | 132 | 10 | 3.6 | 4.4 | 6.5 | 0.3 |
| Spare rib joint, roasted | 90g | 234 | 16 | 6.0 | 0 | 22 | 0 |
| Spare rib joint, roasted, trimmed | 90g | 181 | 8.0 | 2.9 | 0 | 27 | 0 |
| Steaks, grilled | 135g | 267 | 10 | 3.6 | 0 | 44 | 0 |
| Steaks, grilled, trimmed | 135g | 228 | 5.0 | 1.8 | 0 | 46 | 0 |
| **TURKEY** | | | | | | | |
| Breast, grilled, skinned | 100g | 155 | 2.0 | 0.6 | 0 | 35 | 0 |
| Dark meat, roasted | 90g | 159 | 6.0 | 1.8 | 0 | 27 | 0 |
| Drumsticks, roasted | 45g | 84 | 4.0 | 1.2 | 0 | 12 | 0 |
| Light meat, roasted | 90g | 138 | 2.0 | 0.6 | 0 | 30 | 0 |
| Mince, stewed | 100g | 176 | 7.0 | 2.0 | 0 | 29 | 0 |
| Roast turkey | 90g | 154 | 6.0 | 1.9 | 0 | 25 | 0 |
| Thighs, casseroled, skinned | 50g | 91 | 4.0 | 1.3 | 0 | 28 | 0 |
| Turkey slices | 23g | 26 | 0.5 | 0.1 | 0 | 5.3 | 0 |

*No information available Tr trace quantities<0.1g

| Pasta & pasta dishes | Av Portion | Calories | Fat, g | Saturated fat, g | Carbohydrate, g | Protein, g | Fibre, g |
|---|---|---|---|---|---|---|---|
| **PASTA DISHES: ASDA** | | | | | | | |
| Beef lasagne | 400g | 476 | 23 | 11 | 34 | 30 | 5.6 |
| Bolognese pasta bake | 400g | 630 | 24 | 12 | 70 | 30 | 6.0 |
| Chilli pasta bake | 400g | 630 | 20 | 11 | 83 | 28 | 4.0 |
| Roasted vegetable lasagne | 400g | 443 | 20 | 9.6 | 46 | 16 | 4.8 |
| Spinach & ricotta cannelloni | 400g | 595 | 31 | 19 | 55 | 19 | 7.3 |
| **PASTA DISHES: SAINSBURY'S** | | | | | | | |
| Beef lasagne | 400g | 609 | 32 | 16 | 53 | 28 | 6.6 |
| Chicken & bacon pasta bake | 400g | 648 | 33 | 16 | 54 | 31 | 4.1 |
| Spaghetti Bolognese | 400g | 625 | 28 | 11 | 64 | 28 | 6.7 |
| Spaghetti carbonara | 400g | 625 | 29 | 15 | 68 | 21 | 5.2 |
| Spaghetti & meatballs | 400g | 458 | 19 | 6.3 | 43 | 25 | 5.8 |
| Tomato & mozzarella pasta bake | 400g | 495 | 14 | 5.4 | 71 | 19 | 6.0 |
| Vegetable lasagne | 400g | 456 | 23 | 11 | 47 | 11 | 7.6 |
| **PASTA DISHES: TESCO** | | | | | | | |
| Cannelloni, Finest | 360g | 600 | 20 | 12 | 70 | 28 | 11 |
| Chicken & ham pasta bake | 400g | 595 | 18 | 4.4 | 78 | 27 | 4.4 |
| Lasagne al forno, Finest | 400g | 645 | 36 | 14 | 46 | 35 | 6.4 |
| Roasted pepper & spinach lasagne | 350g | 400 | 22 | 10 | 37 | 8.8 | 6.0 |
| Spaghetti Bolognese, Finest | 450g | 705 | 31 | 11 | 65 | 43 | 6.3 |
| Tuna & pasta bake | 400g | 535 | 22 | 11 | 50 | 32 | 4.8 |
| **TINNED PASTA DISHES: HEINZ** | | | | | | | |
| Macaroni cheese | 200g | 174 | 5.9 | 2.1 | 23 | 7.7 | 0.6 |
| Ravioli in tomato sauce | 205g | 155 | 3.3 | 1.2 | 26 | 4.9 | 1.8 |
| Spaghetti hoops in tomato sauce | 200g | 109 | 0.4 | Tr | 23 | 3.5 | 1.2 |
| Spaghetti in tomato sauce | 200g | 120 | 0.5 | Tr | 25 | 3.5 | 4.8 |

| Pastry & savoury pies | Av Portion | Calories | Fat, g | Saturated fat, g | Carbohydrate, g | Protein, g | Fibre, g |
|---|---|---|---|---|---|---|---|
| **PASTRY** | | | | | | | |
| All butter puff pastry, uncooked (Jus Rol) | 50g | 196 | 13 | 9.2 | 17 | 2.8 | 0.7 |
| Filo pastry, (Jus Rol) | 50g | 117 | 1.4 | 0.2 | 26 | 4.0 | 1.1 |
| Puff pastry, uncooked (Jus Rol) | 50g | 214 | 13 | 6.9 | 15 | 2.5 | 0.7 |
| Shortcrust pastry, uncooked (Jus Rol) | 50g | 229 | 15 | 5.6 | 19 | 3.2 | 1.1 |
| **SAVOURY PIES** | | | | | | | |
| Beef pie | 150g | 449 | 29 | 13 | 33 | 11 | * |
| Chicken pie | 130g | 374 | 23 | 9.1 | 32 | 12 | 1.0 |
| Cornish pasty | 155g | 414 | 25 | 9.1 | 39 | 10 | 1.4 |
| Ginsters cheese & onion slice | 180g | 500 | 34 | 18 | 35 | 14 | 5.2 |
| Ginsters Cornish pasty | 227g | 549 | 32 | 15 | 53 | 12 | 7.1 |
| Ginsters large sausage roll | 140g | 499 | 38 | 16 | 27 | 13 | 2.9 |
| Ginsters pepper steak slice | 180g | 455 | 27 | 13 | 38 | 15 | 2.9 |
| Pork & egg pie | 60g | 178 | 13 | 4.4 | 10 | 6.3 | * |
| Pork pie, mini | 50g | 196 | 14 | 5.7 | 13 | 5.3 | 0.5 |
| Pukka Pies all steak pie | 230g | 538 | 33 | 16 | 37 | 23 | 3.7 |
| Pukka Pies chicken & mushroom pie | 230g | 475 | 29 | 11 | 36 | 17 | 8.0 |
| Pukka Pies steak & kidney pie | 230g | 488 | 26 | 12 | 41 | 21 | 8.2 |
| Quiche lorraine, home-made | 140g | 501 | 36 | 15 | 27 | 19 | 1.0 |
| Sausage rolls | 60g | 230 | 17 | 6.7 | 15 | 5.9 | 0.6 |
| Steak & kidney pie, home-made | 120g | 406 | 26 | 9.7 | 27 | 16 | 1.1 |
| Tesco bacon & leek quiche | 100g (¼ quiche) | 230 | 15 | 6.5 | 16 | 6.5 | 3.2 |
| Tesco cheese & onion quiche | 100g (¼ quiche) | 265 | 17 | 7.9 | 17 | 8.8 | 2.5 |
| Tesco quiche lorraine | 100g (¼ quiche) | 175 | 7.7 | 3.2 | 15 | 11 | 3.8 |

| Pizza | Av Portion | Calories | Fat, g | Saturated fat, g | Carbohydrate, g | Protein, g | Fibre, g |
|---|---|---|---|---|---|---|---|
| **CHICAGO TOWN** | | | | | | | |
| Deep dish ham & pineapple | 1 pizza, 170g | 398 | 15 | 7 | 50 | 16 | 2.5 |
| Deep dish meat combo | 1 pizza, 170g | 434 | 19 | 8 | 49 | 18 | 2.5 |
| Takeaway four cheese stuffed crust | ¼ pizza, 157g | 392 | 15 | 8.4 | 47 | 18 | 3.2 |
| Takeaway pepperoni stuffed crust pizza | ¼ pizza, 161g | 428 | 18 | 8.9 | 47 | 19 | 3.2 |
| Ristorante speciale | ½ pizza, 165g | 414 | 21 | 7.6 | 38 | 18 | 3.0 |
| **DR OETKER** | | | | | | | |
| Ristorante Hawaii | ½ pizza, 178g | 382 | 15 | 5.0 | 45 | 15 | 3.0 |
| Ristorante pollo | ½ pizza, 178g | 378 | 16 | 5.5 | 42 | 15 | 3.2 |
| Ristorante quattro formaggi | ½ pizza, 165g | 431 | 23 | 10 | 40 | 18 | 2.6 |
| Ristorante speciale | ½ pizza, 165g | 414 | 21 | 7.6 | 38 | 18 | 3.0 |

*No information available  Tr trace quantities <0.1g

| Pizza | Av Portion | Calories | Fat, g | Saturated fat, g | Carbohydrate, g | Protein, g | Fibre, g |
|---|---|---|---|---|---|---|---|
| **GOODFELLA'S** | | | | | | | |
| Deep loaded cheese | ½ pizza, 209g | 526 | 17 | 10 | 68 | 25 | 4.7 |
| Deep pan pepperoni | ½ pizza, 210g | 538 | 20 | 8.2 | 67 | 23 | 4.2 |
| Flatbread pepperoni speciale | ½ pizza, 207g | 494 | 19 | 8.0 | 58 | 20 | 3.6 |
| Flatbread sweet chilli chicken | ½ pizza, 207g | 530 | 18 | 7.2 | 63 | 26 | 3.8 |
| Stonebaked thin crust roast chicken | ½ pizza, 183g | 442 | 17 | 6.4 | 47 | 26 | 3.6 |
| Stonebaked thin crust vegetable & pesto | ½ pizza, 200g | 382 | 13 | 6.4 | 50 | 16 | 3.6 |
| **PIZZA EXPRESS** | | | | | | | |
| 8in American pizza | ½ pizza, 128g | 303 | 11 | 5.0 | 39 | 13 | 2.8 |
| 8in La Reine pizza | ½ pizza, 142g | 307 | 9.8 | 3.9 | 42 | 13 | 3.7 |
| 8in Lighter Gustosa | ½ pizza, 125g | 220 | 3.9 | 1.6 | 35 | 12 | 4.6 |
| 8in Lighter Vitabella | ½ pizza, 125g | 215 | 3.3 | 2.1 | 39 | 10 | 3.3 |
| 8in Margherita pizza | ½ pizza, 125g | 287 | 8.5 | 1.5 | 40 | 13 | 3.3 |
| 8in Pollo pesto pizza | ½ pizza, 135g | 293 | 5.5 | 2.4 | 46 | 15 | 3.0 |
| 8in Sloppy Giuseppe pizza | ½ pizza, 153g | 306 | 10 | 4.6 | 40 | 13 | 4.6 |
| 12in Margherita pizza | ⅓ pizza, 164g | 374 | 12 | 6.1 | 51 | 17 | 4.4 |

| Puddings | Av Portion | Calories | Fat, g | Saturated fat, g | Carbohydrate, g | Protein, g | Fibre, g |
|---|---|---|---|---|---|---|---|
| Apple crumble | 150g | 311 | 10 | * | 55 | 2.7 | 2.4 |
| Apple pie | 110g slice | 293 | 15 | * | 39 | 3.2 | 1.9 |
| Bakewell tart | 120g slice | 547 | 22 | * | 52 | 7.6 | 2.3 |
| Blancmange | 150g | 171 | 6.0 | 3.4 | 27 | 4.6 | 0 |
| Bread & butter pudding | 150g | 240 | 12 | * | 26 | 9.3 | 0.5 |
| Cheesecake | 100g slice | 426 | 36 | 19 | 25 | 3.7 | 0.4 |
| Chocolate mousse | 60g | 89 | 4.0 | 2.0 | 12 | 2.4 | * |
| Christmas pudding | 100g | 329 | 12 | 6.1 | 56 | 3.0 | 1.7 |
| Crème caramel | 100g | 102 | 2.0 | 0.9 | 21 | 3.0 | * |
| Fruit crumble | 150g | 329 | 12 | 6.0 | 54 | 3.6 | 1.9 |
| Fruit mousse | 60g | 86 | 4.0 | 2.5 | 11 | 2.7 | * |
| Fruit pie | 110g slice | 288 | 15 | 4.6 | 37 | 3.4 | 1.9 |
| Fruit pie, individual | 60g each | 214 | 8.0 | 3.2 | 34 | 2.6 | * |
| Jelly | 125g | 76 | 0 | 0 | 19 | 1.5 | 0 |
| Lemon meringue pie | 80g slice | 201 | 7.0 | 2.5 | 35 | 2.3 | 0.6 |
| Pancakes | 60g each | 181 | 10 | 4.2 | 21 | 3.6 | 0.5 |
| Pavlova | 80g | 230 | 11 | 5.8 | 34 | 2.2 | 0.2 |
| Profiteroles | 90g | 311 | 23 | 13 | 22 | 5.0 | * |
| Rice pudding, canned | 125g | 106 | 2.0 | 0.9 | 20 | 4.1 | 0.1 |
| Rice pudding, canned, low fat | 125g | 89 | 1.0 | 0.6 | 17 | 4.4 | 0.1 |
| Sponge pudding | 110g | 374 | 18 | 5.6 | 50 | 6.4 | 1.2 |
| Spotted dick | 110g | 360 | 18 | * | 47 | 4.6 | 1.1 |
| Treacle tart | 90g slice | 341 | 13 | 3.9 | 57 | 3.5 | 1.0 |
| Trifle | 150g | 249 | 12 | 3.6 | 32 | 3.9 | 0.6 |

| Rice, noodles & rice dishes | Av Portion | Calories | Fat, g | Saturated fat, g | Carbohydrate, g | Protein, g | Fibre, g |
|---|---|---|---|---|---|---|---|
| **RICE & NOODLES** | | | | | | | |
| Arborio rice, uncooked | 60g | 213 | 0.6 | Tr | 47 | 4.1 | 0.3 |
| Basmati rice, uncooked | 60g | 215 | 0.8 | 0.1 | 48 | 4.4 | * |
| Egg noodles, uncooked | 60g | 235 | 5.0 | 1.4 | 43 | 7.3 | 1.7 |
| Noodles, uncooked | 60g | 233 | 4.0 | * | 46 | 7.0 | 1.7 |
| Rice noodles, uncooked | 60g | 216 | Tr | Tr | 49 | 2.9 | * |
| White rice, uncooked | 60g | 217 | 0.5 | 0.1 | 52 | 3.9 | 0.3 |
| Wholegrain rice, uncooked | 60g | 214 | 1.7 | 0.4 | 49 | 4.0 | 1.1 |
| **RICE DISHES** | | | | | | | |
| Gallo Risotto Pronto, four cheese, uncooked | 100g | 347 | 3.0 | * | 72 | 8.0 | * |
| Gallo Risotto Pronto, porcini mushroom, uncooked | 100g | 341 | 1.0 | * | 75 | 8.0 | * |
| Sainsbury's lemon, thyme & chicken risotto | 400g | 514 | 20 | 10 | 43 | 39 | 7.5 |
| Sainsbury's mushroom risotto | 400g | 502 | 22 | 11 | 65 | 8.9 | 2.3 |
| Sainsbury's paella | 400g | 498 | 11 | 2.1 | 69 | 31 | 5.6 |
| Tesco Cook Pot chicken & mushroom risotto | 362g | 650 | 26 | 12 | 66 | 36 | 2.9 |
| Tesco Finest mushroom risotto | 400g | 550 | 27 | 14 | 55 | 16 | 9.6 |
| Tesco Finest paella | 475g | 645 | 24 | 4.7 | 81 | 23 | 6.6 |
| Tesco vegetable paella | 200g | 210 | 8.4 | 1.2 | 30 | 4.6 | 4.2 |
| Uncle Ben's chicken and mushroom risotto | 125g | 223 | 3.9 | 0.8 | 41 | 5.8 | 1.1 |
| Uncle Ben's grilled Mediterranean vegetable risotto | 125g | 206 | 3.0 | 0.6 | 39 | 4.8 | 1.5 |
| Uncle Ben's tomato & Italian herb risotto | 125g | 224 | 5.1 | 1.6 | 39 | 4.6 | 1.6 |
| Waitrose Italian bacon & pea risotto | 350g | 558 | 32 | 13 | 50 | 16 | 3.3 |
| Waitrose Italian roast mushroom risotto | 350g | 434 | 16 | 8.7 | 61 | 9.8 | 2.4 |
| Waitrose Menu for One prawn risotto | 400g | 497 | 20 | 11 | 59 | 19 | 1.4 |
| Waitrose Menu for Two paella | 350g | 484 | 17 | 5.0 | 57 | 3.8 | 4.8 |

| Salads | Av Portion | Calories | Fat, g | Saturated fat, g | Carbohydrate, g | Protein, g | Fibre, g |
|---|---|---|---|---|---|---|---|
| **ASDA** | | | | | | | |
| Carrot & beetroot salad | 160g (1 pack) | 102 | 6.6 | 0.4 | 9.0 | 1.4 | 1.6 |
| Cheese layered salad | 440g (1 pack) | 664 | 34 | * | 62 | 23 | * |
| Mediterranean orzo pasta salad | 280g (1 pack) | 571 | 38 | 3.1 | 49 | 9.0 | 8.7 |
| Prawn layered pasta salad | 197g (1 pack) | 276 | 14 | * | 27 | 9.0 | * |
| Tuna layered pasta salad | 440g (1 pack) | 541 | 21 | * | 56 | 28 | * |
| **BAGGED SALADS** | | | | | | | |
| Baby leaf salad | 100g | 19 | 0.6 | 0.1 | 1.7 | 1.7 | 1.9 |
| Baby spinach | 100g | 25 | 0.8 | 0.1 | 1.6 | 2.8 | 2.1 |
| Caesar salad | 100g | 150 | 13 | 2.6 | 7.0 | 4.9 | 1.1 |
| Lamb's lettuce | 100g | 15 | 0.5 | 0.1 | 1.7 | 0.8 | 0.9 |
| Pea shoots | 100g | 19 | 0.6 | 0.1 | 0.2 | 3.1 | 2.0 |
| Rocket | 100g | 22 | 0.3 | 0.1 | 0.9 | 2.9 | 2.1 |
| Watercress | 100g | 22 | 1.0 | 0.3 | 0.4 | 3.0 | 1.5 |
| Watercress, rocket & spinach salad | 100g | 21 | 0.8 | 0.2 | 1.2 | 2.2 | 1.5 |
| **FLORETTE** | | | | | | | |
| Bistro salad | 100g | 27 | 0.2 | Tr | 3.4 | 1.6 | 2.8 |
| Crispy salad | 100g | 22 | 0.3 | Tr | 3.4 | 1.5 | 3.0 |
| Garden side salad | 110g (1 pack) | 26 | 0.3 | Tr | 3.2 | 1.4 | 2.2 |
| Mixed salad | 100g | 20 | 0.2 | 0.1 | 3.4 | 1.3 | 3.0 |
| **SAINSBURY'S** | | | | | | | |
| Coronation wild rice salad | 300g (1 pack) | 456 | 18 | 3.6 | 66 | 7.2 | 3.0 |
| Giant couscous & feta salad | 220g (1 pack) | 360 | 17 | 3.8 | 36 | 12 | 9.6 |
| Large salad bowl | 80g (1 pack) | 15 | 0.2 | 0.1 | 2.2 | 0.9 | 1.1 |
| Moroccan couscous salad | 200g (1 pack) | 364 | 7.2 | 0.8 | 60 | 8.8 | 11 |
| Rainbow salad | 240g (1 pack) | 286 | 6.8 | 0.8 | 56 | 12 | 5.6 |
| **TESCO** | | | | | | | |
| Caesar salad | 230g (1 pack) | 330 | 22 | 4.6 | 22 | 8.8 | 3.2 |
| Chargrilled chicken pasta snack salad | 275g (1 pack) | 425 | 16 | 2.1 | 49 | 17 | 6.1 |
| Cheese & tomato pasta snack salad | 300g (1 pack) | 545 | 21 | 4.2 | 69 | 17 | 5.1 |
| Chicken & bacon layered salad | 360g (1 pack) | 600 | 40 | 4.0 | 44 | 17 | 6.5 |
| Chilli chicken noodle salad | 230g (1 pack) | 165 | 2.5 | 0.5 | 16 | 19 | 6.9 |
| Honey & mustard chicken pasta snack salad | 350g (1 pack) | 825 | 41 | 5.7 | 87 | 24 | 4.8 |
| Prawn layered salad | 380g (1 pack) | 510 | 28 | 2.3 | 46 | 16 | 6.5 |
| Tuna & sweetcorn snack salad | 350g (1 pack) | 680 | 28 | 2.9 | 79 | 23 | 6.0 |
| **WAITROSE** | | | | | | | |
| Chicken Caesar salad | 250g (1 pack) | 378 | 25 | 5.0 | 15 | 23 | 2.3 |
| Couscous & roasted vegetable salad | 200g (1 pack) | 316 | 10 | 1.2 | 46 | 11 | 2.6 |
| Four bean & buckwheat salad | 220g (1 pack) | 257 | 6.2 | 0.7 | 40 | 11 | 11 |
| Fruity Moroccan couscous salad | 235g (1 pack) | 364 | 8.5 | 0.9 | 60 | 12 | 5.6 |
| Pesto & spinach pasta salad | 190g (1 pack) | 365 | 18 | 3.4 | 40 | 11 | 2.7 |
| Pesto, spinach & pinenut pasta salad | 165g (1 pack) | 339 | 17 | 2.3 | 37 | 6.9 | 2.3 |
| Tomato, basil & chicken pasta salad | 205g (1 pack) | 310 | 25 | 3.5 | 37 | 17 | 2.3 |
| Tuna niçoise salad | 330g (1 pack) | 343 | 22 | 3.3 | 17 | 18 | 3.0 |

| Sauces & dressings | Av Portion | Calories | Fat, g | Saturated fat, g | Carbohydrate, g | Protein, g | Fibre, g |
|---|---|---|---|---|---|---|---|
| Apple chutney | 30g (1 tbsp) | 57 | 0 | 0 | 15 | 0.3 | 0.4 |
| Barbecue sauce | 20g (1 tbsp) | 19 | 0 | 0 | 4.7 | 0.2 | 0.1 |
| Branston pickle, Crosse & Blackwell | 30g (1 tbsp) | 33 | 0.1 | 0 | 7.8 | 0.2 | 0.3 |
| Brown sauce | 20g (1 tbsp) | 20 | 0 | 0 | 5.0 | 0.2 | 0.1 |
| Chilli sauce | 20g (1 tbsp) | 16 | 0 | 0 | 3.5 | 0.3 | 0.2 |
| French dressing | 15g (1 tbsp) | 98 | 11 | 1.5 | 0 | 0 | 0 |
| Horseradish sauce | 20g (1 tbsp) | 31 | 2.0 | 0.2 | 3.6 | 0.5 | 0.5 |
| Light mayonnaise, Hellmann's | 30g (1 tbsp) | 88 | 8.9 | 0.9 | 2.0 | 0.2 | 0 |
| Mango chutney | 30g (1 tbsp) | 57 | 0 | 0 | 15 | 0.2 | * |
| Mayonnaise | 30g (1 tbsp) | 207 | 23 | 3.4 | 0.5 | 0.3 | 0 |
| Salad cream | 20g (1 tbsp) | 70 | 6.0 | 0.7 | 3.3 | 0.3 | 0 |
| Soy sauce | 15g (1 tbsp) | 10 | 0 | 0 | 1.2 | 0.8 | 0 |
| Tomato ketchup | 20g (1 tbsp) | 23 | 0 | 0 | 5.7 | 0.3 | 0.2 |
| **PASTA SAUCE** | | | | | | | |
| Bertolli pasta sauce with basil | 100g | 71 | 4.6 | 0.6 | 5.4 | 1.5 | 1.2 |
| Dolmio bolognese | 100g | 50 | 1.3 | 0.2 | 7.3 | 1.5 | 1.3 |
| Lloyd Grossman tomato & chilli | 100g | 88 | 5.7 | 0.7 | 7.3 | 1.7 | 0.9 |
| Seeds of Change tomato & basil | 100g | 59 | 2.0 | 0.4 | 9.0 | 1.2 | 0.8 |
| **PESTO SAUCE** | | | | | | | |
| Sacla classic green pesto | 25g | 138 | 11 | 1.1 | 1.0 | 1.4 | 1.3 |
| Sacla sundried tomato pesto | 25g | 76 | 7.3 | 1.1 | 1.4 | 1.1 | 1.1 |
| White sauce for lasagne, Dolmio | 100g | 98 | 7.5 | 2.8 | 6.9 | 0.5 | |

*No information available  Tr trace quantities <0.1g

| Soups | Av Portion | Calories | Fat, g | Saturated fat, g | Carbohydrate, g | Protein, g | Fibre, g |
|---|---|---|---|---|---|---|---|
| **BATCHELORS CUP A SOUP** | | | | | | | |
| Chicken & vegetable | 27.5g (1 sachet) | 137 | 6.6 | 3.3 | 18 | 1.3 | 2.2 |
| Minestrone | 23.5g (1 sachet) | 93 | 1.8 | 0.9 | 17 | 1.9 | 1.3 |
| Mushroom | 24g (1 sachet) | 123 | 6.3 | 3.7 | 15 | 1.1 | 0.5 |
| Tomato | 23.3g (1 sachet) | 90 | 2.1 | 1.1 | 16 | 0.9 | 0.8 |
| **BAXTERS** | | | | | | | |
| Country garden | 200g (½ can) | 73 | 1.2 | 0.6 | 14 | 1.9 | 1.7 |
| Lentil & vegetable | 200g (½ can) | 87 | 0.4 | 0.1 | 16 | 4.8 | 2.3 |
| Oxtail | 200g (½ can) | 93 | 2.7 | 0.6 | 13 | 3.9 | 1.0 |
| Scotch broth | 200g (½ can) | 96 | 2.0 | 0.8 | 16 | 4.0 | 1.3 |
| **HEINZ** | | | | | | | |
| Cream of chicken | 200g (½ can) | 105 | 6.0 | 1.0 | 9.4 | 3.4 | 0.2 |
| Cream of mushroom | 200g (½ can) | 106 | 5.5 | 0.8 | 11 | 3.4 | 0.3 |
| Cream of tomato | 200g (½ can) | 113 | 5.9 | 0.4 | 13 | 1.8 | 0.8 |
| Vegetable | 200g (½ can) | 89 | 1.7 | 0.1 | 16 | 2.2 | 1.8 |
| **NEW COVENT GARDEN** | | | | | | | |
| Broccoli & Stilton | 300g (½ carton) | 167 | 11 | 6.9 | 8.1 | 8.7 | 3.3 |
| Carrot & coriander | 300g (½ carton) | 129 | 6.6 | 3.9 | 16 | 1.8 | 3.6 |
| Leek & potato | 300g (½ carton) | 150 | 6.0 | 3.6 | 20 | 3.6 | 2.4 |
| Minestrone | 300g (½ carton) | 111 | 2.7 | 0.3 | 17 | 4.2 | 3.6 |
| Spicy butternut squash & sweet potato | 300g (½ carton) | 192 | 11 | 4.5 | 21 | 3.0 | 3.0 |
| Tomato & basil | 300g (½ carton) | 132 | 6.0 | 0.9 | 16 | 3.9 | 3.9 |
| **WEIGHT WATCHERS** | | | | | | | |
| Carrot & lentil | 295g (1 can) | 86 | 0.4 | 0.1 | 17 | 3.8 | 2.1 |
| Chicken | 295g (1 can) | 98 | 3.1 | 0.4 | 13 | 4.7 | 0.1 |
| Tomato | 295g (1 can) | 74 | 1.4 | 0.1 | 13 | 2.0 | 0.8 |

| Storecupboard ingredients | Av Portion | Calories | Fat, g | Saturated fat, g | Carbohydrate, g | Protein, g | Fibre, g |
|---|---|---|---|---|---|---|---|
| **HERBS & SPICES** | | | | | | | |
| Balsamic vinegar | 15g (1 tbsp) | 10 | 0 | 0 | 2.5 | Tr | 0 |
| Basil, dried | 1g (1 tsp) | 3 | 0 | 0 | 0.4 | 0.1 | * |
| Curry powder | 2g (1 tsp) | 5 | 0 | 0 | 0.5 | 0.2 | 0.5 |
| Mixed herbs | 2g (1 tsp) | 5 | 0 | 0 | 0.7 | 0.2 | * |
| Mustard powder | 3g (1 tsp) | 14 | 1.0 | 0 | 0.6 | 0.9 | * |
| Mustard, smooth | 8g (1 tsp) | 11 | 1.0 | 0 | 0.8 | 0.6 | * |
| Mustard, wholegrain | 8g (1 tsp) | 11 | 1.0 | 0 | 0.3 | 0.7 | 0.4 |
| Salt | 5g (1 tsp) | 0 | 0 | 0 | 0 | 0 | 0 |
| Stock cubes, Oxo, beef | 7g (1 cube) | 19 | 0.4 | Tr | 3.0 | 1.1 | Tr |
| Stock cubes, Oxo, vegetable | 7g (1 cube) | 18 | 0.3 | 0.2 | 2.9 | 0.7 | 0.1 |
| Tomato purée | 20g (1 tbsp) | 15 | 0 | 0 | 2.8 | 1.0 | 0.6 |
| Vegetable bouillon powder, Marigold | 5g (1 tsp) | 12 | 0.4 | 0.2 | 1.5 | 0.5 | Tr |
| Vinegar | 15 (1 tbsp) | 3 | 0 | 0 | 0.1 | 0.1 | 0 |
| **FLOURS** | | | | | | | |
| Cornflour | 20g (1 tbsp) | 71 | 0 | 0 | 18 | 0.1 | 0 |
| Flour, white, bread | 20g (1 tbsp) | 68 | 0 | 0 | 15 | 2.3 | 0.6 |
| Flour, white, plain | 20g (1 tbsp) | 68 | 0 | 0 | 16 | 1.9 | 0.6 |
| Flour, white, self-raising | 20g (1 tbsp) | 66 | 0 | 0 | 15 | 1.8 | 0.6 |
| Flour, wholemeal | 20g (1 tbsp) | 62 | 0 | 0 | 13 | 2.5 | 1.8 |
| **SUGARS** | | | | | | | |
| Golden syrup | 20g (1 tbsp) | 60 | 0 | 0 | 16 | 0.1 | 0 |
| Sugar, brown | 5g (1 tsp) | 18 | 0 | 0 | 5.1 | 0 | 0 |
| Sugar, icing | 15g (1 tbsp) | 59 | 0 | 0 | 16 | 0 | 0 |
| Sugar, white | 5g (1 tsp) | 20 | 0 | 0 | 5.3 | 0 | 0 |

| Vegetables | Av Portion | Calories | Fat, g | Saturated fat, g | Carbohydrate, g | Protein, g | Fibre, g |
|---|---|---|---|---|---|---|---|
| Asparagus | 80g | 20 | 0.6 | 0.1 | 1.6 | 2.3 | 1.4 |
| Aubergine | 80g | 12 | 0.3 | 0.1 | 1.8 | 0.7 | 1.6 |
| Beansprouts | 80g | 25 | 0.4 | 0.1 | 3.2 | 2.3 | 1.2 |
| Beetroot | 80g | 29 | 0.1 | Tr | 6.1 | 1.4 | 1.5 |
| Broccoli | 80g | 26 | 1.0 | 0.2 | 1.4 | 3.5 | 2.1 |
| Broccoli, sprouting | 80g | 28 | 1.0 | 0.2 | 2.1 | 3.1 | 2.8 |
| Brussels sprouts | 80g | 34 | 1.0 | 0.2 | 3.3 | 2.8 | 3.3 |
| Cabbage | 80g | 21 | 1.0 | 0.1 | 3.3 | 1.4 | 1.9 |
| Cabbage, red | 80g | 17 | 0.3 | Tr | 3.0 | 0.9 | 2.0 |
| Carrots | 80g | 28 | 0.3 | 0.1 | 6.3 | 0.5 | 1.9 |
| Cauliflower | 80g | 27 | 1.0 | 0.2 | 2.4 | 2.9 | 1.4 |
| Celeriac | 80g | 14 | 0.3 | * | 1.8 | 1.0 | 3.0 |
| Celery | 30g (1 stick) | 2 | Tr | 0 | 0.3 | 0.2 | 0.3 |

| Vegetables | Av Portion | Calories | Fat, g | Saturated fat, g | Carbohydrate, g | Protein, g | Fibre, g |
|---|---|---|---|---|---|---|---|
| Courgette | 80g | 14 | 0.3 | 0.1 | 1.4 | 1.4 | 0.7 |
| Cucumber | 25g (6 slices) | 3 | Tr | 0 | 0.4 | 0.2 | 0.2 |
| Curly kale | 80g | 26 | 1.0 | 0.2 | 1.1 | 2.7 | 2.5 |
| Fennel | 80g | 10 | 1.3 | 0.2 | 1.4 | 0.7 | 1.9 |
| Garlic | 3g (1 clove) | 3 | Tr | 0 | 0.5 | 0.2 | 0.1 |
| Ginger | 5g | 2 | Tr | 0 | 0.5 | 0.1 | * |
| Green beans | 80g | 18 | 1.0 | 0.1 | 2.3 | 1.4 | 1.9 |
| Leeks | 80g | 18 | 1.0 | 0.1 | 2.3 | 1.3 | 1.8 |
| Lettuce | 20g | 3 | Tr | 0 | 0.3 | 0.2 | 0.2 |
| Marrow | 80g | 10 | Tr | 0 | 1.8 | 0.4 | 0.4 |
| Mushrooms | 80g | 10 | 1.0 | 0.1 | 0.3 | 1.4 | 0.9 |
| Onions | 120g (one) | 43 | Tr | 0 | 9.5 | 1.4 | 1.7 |
| Parsnips | 80g | 51 | 1.0 | 0.1 | 10 | 1.4 | 3.7 |
| Parsnips, roast | 80g | 91 | 5.0 | Tr | 10 | 1.3 | 3.8 |
| Peas, frozen | 80g | 53 | 1.0 | 0.2 | 7.4 | 4.6 | 4.1 |
| Peppers, green | 160g (one) | 24 | 1.0 | 0.2 | 4.2 | 1.3 | 2.6 |
| Peppers, red | 160g (one) | 51 | 1.0 | 0.2 | 10 | 1.6 | 2.6 |
| Peppers, yellow | 160g (one) | 42 | Tr | Tr | 8.5 | 1.9 | 2.7 |
| Plantain | 150g (one) | 176 | 1.0 | 0.2 | 44 | 1.7 | 1.9 |
| Potatoes, baked | 180g (one) | 94 | 0.4 | Tr | 22 | 2.7 | 1.6 |
| Potatoes, boiled | 180g | 130 | 0.1 | Tr | 31 | 3.2 | 2.2 |
| Potatoes, chips, home-made | 165g | 312 | 11 | 1.0 | 50 | 6.4 | 3.6 |
| Potatoes, chips, frozen, fried | 165g | 450 | 22 | 2.0 | 59 | 6.8 | 4.0 |
| Potatoes, mashed with margarine | 120g | 125 | 5.0 | 1.1 | 19 | 2.2 | 1.3 |
| Potatoes, new | 80g | 60 | 1.0 | 0.1 | 14 | 1.2 | 0.9 |
| Potatoes, roast | 130g | 194 | 6.0 | 0.8 | 34 | 3.8 | 2.3 |
| Potatoes, oven chips, frozen, baked | 165g | 259 | 7.0 | 2.8 | 46 | 5.3 | 3.0 |
| Pumpkin | 80g | 10 | 1.0 | 0.1 | 1.8 | 0.6 | 0.8 |
| Radishes | 8g (one) | 1 | Tr | 0 | 0.2 | 0.1 | 0.1 |
| Runner beans | 80g | 18 | 1.0 | 0.1 | 2.6 | 1.3 | 1.6 |
| Spinach | 80g | 20 | 1.0 | 0.1 | 1.3 | 2.2 | 1.7 |
| Spring greens | 80g | 26 | 1.0 | 0.1 | 1.3 | 2.2 | 1.7 |
| Spring onions | 10g (one) | 2 | Tr | 0 | 0.3 | 0.2 | 0.2 |
| Squash, butternut | 80g | 29 | Tr | 0 | 6.6 | 0.9 | 1.3 |
| Swede | 80g | 19 | Tr | 0 | 4.0 | 0.6 | 1.5 |
| Sweet potatoes | 180g (one) | 157 | 1.0 | 0.2 | 2.2 | 2.0 | 1.6 |
| Sweetcorn, canned | 80g | 98 | 1.0 | 0.2 | 21 | 2.3 | 1.1 |
| Tomatoes, canned | 200g (½ can) | 32 | Tr | 0 | 6.0 | 2.0 | 1.4 |
| Tomatoes | 85g (one) | 14 | 1.0 | 0.1 | 2.6 | 0.6 | 0.9 |

| Vegetarian products | Av Portion | Calories | Fat, g | Saturated fat, g | Carbohydrate, g | Protein, g | Fibre, g |
|---|---|---|---|---|---|---|---|
| **QUORN** | | | | | | | |
| Broccoli & cheese escalopes | 120g (1 escalope) | 251 | 14 | 3.5 | 20 | 10 | 3.5 |
| Chicken-style pieces | 75g (¼ pack) | 86 | 2.0 | 0.5 | 4.3 | 11 | 4.3 |
| Cottage pie | 250g | 167 | 2.5 | 1.3 | 28 | 6.3 | 4.5 |
| Crispy nuggets | 17g (1 nugget) | 33 | 2.0 | 0.2 | 1.4 | 2.0 | 0.8 |
| Family roast | 91g (⅛ pack) | 96 | 1.8 | 0.4 | 4.1 | 14 | 4.4 |
| Fajita strips | 70g (½ pack) | 69 | 1.1 | 0.2 | 4.9 | 9.8 | 3.5 |
| Fillets | 52g (1 fillet) | 55 | 0.8 | 0.1 | 2.6 | 6.8 | 2.6 |
| Fishless fingers | 28.5g (1 finger) | 66 | 3.0 | 0.5 | 6.3 | 2.9 | 1.4 |
| Mince | 75g (¼ pack) | 79 | 1.5 | 0.4 | 3.4 | 11 | 4.1 |
| Mini sausage rolls | 18g (1 roll) | 48 | 2.2 | 0.8 | 4.3 | 2.8 | 0.5 |
| Mozzarella & pesto escalope | 120g (1 escalope) | 260 | 16 | 4.0 | 18 | 12 | 5.4 |
| Peppered steaks | 98g (1 steak) | 115 | 3.7 | 0.5 | 7.3 | 11 | 3.9 |
| Pieces | 87.5g (¼ pack) | 100 | 2.3 | 0.5 | 5.1 | 12 | 4.8 |
| Smoky bacon-style slices | 37.5g ¼ pack) | 82 | 6.1 | 0.7 | 1.1 | 4.6 | 2.7 |
| Steak strips | 75G (¼ pack) | 81 | 1.8 | 0.8 | 3.2 | 11 | 4.5 |
| **TOFU** | | | | | | | |
| Cauldron organic tofu mince | 100g | 189 | 11 | 2.6 | 2.5 | 19 | 1.9 |
| Cauldron original tofu | 100g | 85 | 4.2 | 0.7 | 1.9 | 10 | 0.9 |
| Cauldron marinated tofu pieces | 80g (½ pack) | 182 | 14 | 2.0 | 0.8 | 14 | 2.2 |

| Vegetarian products | Av Portion | Calories | Fat, g | Saturated fat, g | Carbohydrate, g | Protein, g | Fibre, g |
|---|---|---|---|---|---|---|---|
| **VEGETARIAN BURGERS** | | | | | | | |
| Cauldron mushroom burgers | 87.5g 1 burger) | 150 | 7.0 | 0.4 | 14 | 7.0 | 1.3 |
| Linda McCartney cranberry & camembert burgers | 88g | 250 | 14 | 1.4 | 11 | 19 | 4.7 |
| Linda McCartney mozzarella burger | 90g (1 burger) | 233 | 15 | 2.2 | 8.7 | 19 | 3.7 |
| Linda McCartney vegetarian burgers | 50g ( 1 burger) | 62 | 1.5 | 0.5 | 5.4 | 7.9 | 2.9 |
| Quorn burgers southern-style | 63g (1 burger) | 123 | 6.2 | 0.8 | 9.1 | 6.7 | 1.9 |
| Quorn sizzling burgers | 80g (1 burger) | 128 | 4.8 | 2.4 | 5.6 | 14 | 2.4 |
| Tesco meat-free Mexican-style bean burgers | 105g (1 burger) | 225 | 9.2 | 0.5 | 25 | 6.0 | 7.6 |
| Tesco meat-free vegetable quarterpounders | 105g (1 burger) | 210 | 8.9 | 0.9 | 27 | 3.6 | 3.3 |
| Tesco vegelicious bean burgers | 75g (1 burger) | 126 | 4.5 | 0.5 | 7.0 | 14 | 1.5 |
| **VEGETARIAN READY MEALS** | | | | | | | |
| Cauldron falafel | 100g (½ pack) | 305 | 19 | 1.6 | 23 | 7.5 | 6.0 |
| Linda McCartney cannelloni | 375g | 386 | 12 | 6.4 | 50 | 13 | 3.7 |
| Linda McCartney lasagne | 360g | 450 | 20 | 10 | 45 | 23 | 5.2 |
| Linda McCartney vegetarian farmhouse pies | 146g (1 pie) | 379 | 23 | 11 | 34 | 8.5 | 2.4 |
| Linda McCartney vegetarian roast | 113g | 227 | 12 | 0.9 | 7.6 | 21 | 0.7 |
| Tesco meat-free cauliflower cheese grills | 92.7g (1 grill) | 220 | 12 | 3.2 | 22 | 5.2 | 2.2 |
| Tesco meat-free nut cutlets | 70g (1 cutlet) | 240 | 16 | 2.1 | 16 | 5.6 | 2.7 |
| Tesco meat-free vegetable fingers | 49g (2 fingers) | 110 | 4.9 | 0.5 | 13 | 1.8 | 1.8 |
| **VEGETARIAN SAUSAGES** | | | | | | | |
| Cauldron Lincolnshire sausages | 50g (1 sausage) | 79 | 4.4 | 0.3 | 2.0 | 7.8 | 1.3 |
| Garden Gourmet vegetarian hot dogs | 70g (2 sausages) | 173 | 11 | 1.3 | 4.9 | 13 | 1.1 |
| Linda McCartney Italian vegetarian sausages | 100g (2 sausages) | 152 | 5.6 | 3.1 | 6.9 | 17 | 3.4 |
| Linda McCartney original sausages | 50g (1 sausage) | 101 | 4.4 | 1.8 | 4.1 | 11 | 0.8 |
| Quorn Cumberland sausages | 50g (1 sausage) | 86 | 3.5 | 0.3 | 6.0 | 6.8 | 1.8 |
| Quorn sausages | 42g (1 sausage) | 70 | 2.9 | 0.3 | 4.9 | 5.3 | 1.5 |

# Index

alcoholic drinks, calorie counter 203
almond, with baked apricot 72
American Journal of Clinical Nutrition 8
anchovy
  chicken Caesar salad 156–7
  crispy-crumbed cabbage pasta 190–1
appetite control 11
apple
  and blueberry strudel 70–1
  compote 73
  easy peasy pork chops 176–7
  galette 140–1
  slaw 108–9
apricot
  baked, with almonds 72
  tropical fruit pots 14
artichoke, goat's cheese & onion slice 196–7
asparagus
  Milanese risotto with wrapped monkfish 186–7
  zingy fish 56–7
aubergine
  griddled polenta ratatouille stack 194–5
summer couscous 162–3
avocado
  Cajun fish wraps 114–15
  grilled, tomato & mozzarella salad 98–9

bacon
  calorie counter 224
  mulligatawny soup 152–3
  Scotch broth 154–5
  Spanish omelette 146–7
  Sunday brunch bake 84–5
bakery, calorie counter 207
banana
  breakfast bruschetta 20
  cake 142
barbecue sauce with turkey meatballs 168–9
bean sprout(s)
  beef pho 88–9
  easy veggie pad Thai 192–3
  sprouted bean and mango salad 46
bean(s) 11
  broad, & feta salad 44–5
  calorie counter 200–37
  Mexican chicken stew 102–3
  and mushroom hotpot 134–5
  on toast 82–3
  see also butter bean; cannellini bean; green bean; kidney bean
beef
  calorie counter 224
  chilli, noodle salad 40–1
  and dumpling stew 182–3
  fajitas 180–1
  goulash soup 90–1

pho 88–9
berries
  berry breakfast 17
  summer pudding 68–9
  toasted oats 80–1
  see also blueberry; raspberry; strawberry
beta-carotene 12
biscuits, calorie counter 205–6
black-eyed bean, Mexican chicken stew 102–3
blood pressure, high 10, 11
blueberry
  and apple strudel 70–1
  berry breakfast 17
  breakfast bruschetta 20
  exotic fruit salad 136–7
  toasted oats 80–1
body fat, calorie content 8
borlotti bean, on toast 82–3
bread 11
  breakfast bruschetta 20
  and butter pudding 198
  calorie counter 207
  deluxe fig and ham salad 38–9
  low-fat corn bread 92–3
  panzanella salad 47
  summer pudding 68–9
  white bean salad 101
  zingy fish 56–7
  see also toast
breakfast cereals, calorie counter 208–9
broad bean and feta salad 44–5
broccoli see tenderstem broccoli
bruschetta, breakfast 20
bulgur wheat and salmon pilau 112–13
buns, calorie counter 209
Burger King, calorie counter 216
burgers, Moroccan lamb 172–3
butter, hazelnut 188–9
butter bean
  mash 130–1
  salad 101
butternut squash
  risotto, with hazelnut butter 188–9
  soup, with cheesy toasts 34–5

cabbage
  crispy-crumbed pasta 190–1
  see also red cabbage
Caesar chicken salad 156–7
Café Nero, calorie counter 216
Cajun fish wraps 114–15
cakes
  banana 142
  calorie counter 208–9
  courgette 143
  raspberry and peach 199
calcium 12
calorie allowance, daily 9
calorie counter 200–37
calorie expenditure, daily 9
calorie reduction ideas 9

calorie swaps, easy 9
calorie(s), definition 9
cannellini bean
  minestrone 32–3
  and potato, spicy 51
  salad 101
  sausage & gnocchi one-pan 110–11
  on toast 82–3
carbohydrates 8, 9, 10
cheese
  calorie counter 210
  cheesy chicken cobbler 104–5
  cheesy polenta with tomato sauce 62
  cheesy toasts, with butternut squash soup 34–5
  griddled polenta ratatouille stack 194–5
  see also goat's cheese; mozzarella; Parmesan
chicken
  Caesar salad 156–7
  calorie counter 224
  cheesy cobbler 104–5
  chow mein 164–5
  and dumpling soup 26–7
  harissa, & couscous salad 94–5
  Mexican stew 102–3
  mulligatawny soup 152–3
  paella 166–7
  tagine 52–3
  tarragon sweet potatoes 106–7
  throw-it-all-together salad 36–7
  chickpea on toast 82–3
chilli
  beef noodle salad 40–1
  crab noodles 118–19
  chilli (dish), lentil 132–3
Chinese restaurants, calorie counter 216
chocolate soufflés 66–7
cholesterol
  high blood levels 10
  LDL ('bad') 10, 11
chow mein, chicken 164–5
chowder, healthy fish 30–1
cobbler, cheesy chicken 104–5
coconut yogurt, tropical fruit pots 14
cod, crusted, with minted pea mash 58–9
coleslaw, crunchy 170–1
compote, apple 73
confectionary, calorie counter 212–13
corn bread, low-fat 92–3
courgette
  blonde pizza 124–5
  cake 143
  and goat's cheese spaghetti 122–3
  griddled polenta ratatouille stack 194–5

Milanese risotto with wrapped monkfish 186–7
white bean salad 101
couscous
  chicken tagine 52–3
  salad, & harissa chicken 94–5
  summer 162–3
crab chilli noodles 118–19
cream, calorie counter 210
crisps, calorie counter 214–15
crispy-crumbed cabbage pasta 190–1
croûtons 42–3, 156–7
cucumber, Greek pasta salad 100

dairy foods 11
diabetes type 2 10
dressings 36–7, 42–3, 156–7
  calorie counter 232
  Thai 40–1
dried fruit
  chicken tagine 52–3
  with porridge 19
dumplings
  and beef stew 182–3
  and chicken soup 26–7

eating out, calorie counter 216–18
eatwell plate 11
egg 11
  Benedict 148–9
  calorie counter 218
  easy veggie pad Thai 192–3
  French toast 21
  griddled polenta ratatouille stack 194–5
  huevos rancheros 24–5
  poached, with mushrooms 22–3
  smoked haddock kedgeree 150–1
  Spanish omelette 146–7
  Sunday brunch bake 84–5
  vegetable frittata 64–5
elderflower and raspberry jelly 74–5
energy drinks, calorie counter 203
escalopes, pork, and apple slaw 108–9
essential fatty acids 10

fajitas, beef 180–1
fat, body 8
fat, dietary 8, 10
  calorie counter 219
  monounsaturated 10
  polyunsaturated 10
  saturated 8, 10
  trans 10
  unsaturated 10
feta
  and broad bean salad 44–5
  Greek pasta salad 100

fibre 8, 10–11
  insoluble 11
  soluble 11
fig and ham deluxe salad 38–9
filo pastry, apple & blueberry
  strudel 70–1
fish 11
  Cajun wraps 114–15
  calorie counter 220
  and chips, calorie counter 216
  healthy chowder 30–1
  smoked mackerel superfood
    salad 96–7
  wrapped monkfish with
    Milanese risotto 186–7
  zingy 56–7
  see also haddock, smoked;
    salmon; sardine
  fish products, calorie counter
    221
fizzy drinks, calorie counter 204
flour, calorie counter 234
folic acid 12
food labels 13
Food Standards Agency (FSA) 13
French toast 21
frittata, vegetable 64–5
fruit 11
  calorie counter 222–3
  exotic salad 136–7
  fruity rice pudding 138–9
  see also dried fruit; specific
    fruit

galette, apple 140–1
game, calorie counter 225
gammon and pea soup 86–7
GDAs see Guideline Daily
  Amounts
ginger, preserved, tropical fruit
  pots 14
gnocchi & sausage one-pan
  110–11
goat's cheese
  and courgette spaghetti 122–3
  and onion slice 196–7
  and sunblush tomato pasta 185
goulash soup 90–1
Greek pasta salad 100
green bean(s)
  deluxe fig and ham salad 38–9
  hot smoked salmon salad 42–3
  warm spiced salad Niçoise
    158–9
Guideline Daily Amounts
  (GDAs) 13
gumbo, prawn 116–17

haddock, smoked
  healthy fish chowder 30–1
  kedgeree 150–1
halloumi and quinoa salad 160–1
ham
  calorie counter 225
  and fig deluxe salad 38–9
  and pea soup 86–7
  see also Parma ham
harissa chicken and couscous
  salad 94–5
hazelnut butter, with squash
  risotto 188–9

healthy diet 10–12
heart disease 10, 11
herbs, calorie counter 234
high blood pressure 10, 11
hot drinks, calorie counter 204
huevos rancheros 24–5
hunger pangs, reduction 11

ice cream
  calorie counter 213
  three-ingredient strawberry 77
icing 142, 143
Indian restaurants, calorie
  counter 216
ingredient lists 13
Irish stew 174–5
iron 12

JD Wetherspoon, calorie counter
  217
jelly, raspberry and elderflower
  74–5

kebabs, lamb spiced, with
  crunchy coleslaw 170–1
kedgeree, smoked haddock
  150–1
KFC, calorie counter 217
kidney bean
  lentil chilli 132–3
  and rice, with sticky ribs 178–9
kilojoules, definition 9
kilokalories, definition 9

lamb
  calorie counter 225
  Irish stew 174–5
  Moroccan burgers 172–3
  Scotch broth 154–5
  spiced kebabs, with crunchy
    coleslaw 170–1
leek, prawn and pea creamy
  penne 120–1
lemon sorbet 76
lentil
  calorie counter 200–37
  chilli 132–3
  red, soup, with low-fat corn
    bread 92–3
  smoked mackerel superfood
    salad 96–7
low fat diets 10

McDonald's, calorie counter
  217
mackerel, smoked, superfood
  salad 96–7
magnesium 12
mango
  exotic fruit salad 136–7
  and sprouted bean salad 46
  tropical fruit pots 14
mash, butter bean 130–1
meat 11
  calorie counter 224–6
  meatballs, turkey, with
    barbecue sauce 168–9
melon, exotic fruit salad 136–7
Mexican chicken stew 102–3
Milanese risotto with wrapped
  monkfish 186–7

milk 11
  calorie counter 211
minerals 12
minestrone, warming veggie
  32–3
monkfish, wrapped, with
  Milanese risotto 186–7
Moroccan lamb burgers 172–3
mozzarella
  blonde pizza 124–5
  grilled avocado & tomato
    salad 98–9
  mushrooms 50
  white bean salad 101
  mozzarella mushrooms 50
muffins
  Sunday brunch bake 84–5
mulligatawny soup 152–3
mushroom
  and bean hotpot 134–5
  mozzarella 50
  with poached egg 22–3
  and two-grain risotto 126–7
mussel, paella 166–7

Niçoise salad, warm spiced
  158–9
noodle(s)
  calorie counter 230
  chicken chow mein 164–5
  chilli crab 118–19
  easy veggie pad Thai 192–3
  salad, chilli beef 40–1
nutrition claims 13
nutrition labels 13
nut(s), calorie counter 200–37

oat(s)
  porridge with dried fruit 19
  toasted, with berries 80–1
offal, calorie counter 226
oils, calorie counter 219
okra, prawn gumbo 116–17
olive, black, penne puttanesca
  184
omega-3 fatty acids 10
omega-6 fatty acids 10
omelette, Spanish 146–7
orange
  exotic fruit salad 136–7
  tropical fruit pots 14

pad Thai, easy veggie 192–3
paella 166–7
panzanella salad 47
pappardelle, with rabbit ragu
  54–5
Parma ham, wrapped monkfish
  with Milanese risotto 186–7
Parmesan
  cheesy polenta with tomato
    sauce 62
  Milanese risotto with
    wrapped monkfish 186–7
pasta 11
  calorie counter 227
  courgette & goat's cheese
    spaghetti 122–3
  crispy-crumbed cabbage
    190–1
  goat's cheese and sunblush

tomatoes 185
  Greek salad 100
penne puttanesca 184
  prawn and pea creamy penne
    120–1
  rabbit ragu with pappardelle
    54–5
pasta sauce, calorie counter 232
pastries, calorie counter 209
pastry, calorie counter 228
pea
  and ham soup 86–7
  Milanese risotto with
    wrapped monkfish 186–7
  minted mash 58–9
  and prawn creamy penne
    120–1
  quinoa and halloumi salad
    60–1
  salmon and bulgur wheat
    pilau 112–13
  Scotch broth 154–5
peach & raspberry cake 199
pearl barley, Scotch broth 154–5
penne
  creamy prawn and pea 120–1
  puttanesca 184
pepper
  beef fajitas 180–1
  Cajun fish wraps 114–15
  easy veggie pad Thai 192–3
  griddled polenta ratatouille
    stack 194–5
  huevos rancheros 24–5
  Mexican chicken stew 102–3
  mozzarella mushrooms 50
  paella 166–7
  pasta, goat's cheese and
    sunblush tomato 185
  prawn & pineapple skewers
    60–1
  prawn gumbo 116–17
  red, and saffron risotto 128–9
  summer couscous 162–3
  vegetable frittata 64–5
pesto sauce, calorie counter 232
pho, beef 88–9
pies, calorie counter 228
pilau, salmon and bulgur wheat
  112–13
pineapple
  exotic fruit salad 136–7
  and prawn skewers 60–1
  tropical fruit pots 14
pistachio, courgette cake 143
pizza
  blonde 124–5
  calorie counter 228–9
  Pizza Hut, calorie counter 217
polenta
  cheesy, with tomato sauce 62
  griddled, ratatouille stack
    194–5
pomegranate seeds, smoked
  mackerel superfood salad
    96–7
pork
  calorie counter 226
  easy peasy chops 176–7
  escalopes, and apple slaw
    108–9

sticky ribs with rice and beans 178–9
porridge with dried fruit 19
portion sizes 11
potassium 12
potato 11
and bean, spicy 51
easy peasy chops pork 176–7
goulash soup 90–1
healthy fish chowder 30–1
hot smoked salmon salad 42–3
Irish stew 174–5
Spanish omelette 146–7
warm spiced salad Niçoise 158–9
prawn
gumbo 116–17
and pea creamy penne 120–1
and pineapple skewers 60–1
protein 8, 9, 10, 11
puddings, calorie counter 229
puttanesca, penne 184

quark cheese, breakfast bruschetta 20
quinoa
and halloumi salad 160–1
mushroom & two-grain risotto 126–7
Quorn 236

rabbit ragu with pappardelle 54–5
raspberry
conserve, berry breakfast 17
and elderflower jelly 74–5
and peach cake 199
ratatouille griddled polenta stack 194–5
red cabbage
apple slaw 108–9
crunchy coleslaw 170–1
white bean salad 101
rib(s), sticky, with rice & beans 178–9
rice 11
and beans, with sticky ribs 178–9
butternut squash risotto with hazelnut butter 188–9
calorie counter 230
fruity rice pudding 138–9
Mexican chicken stew 102–3
Milanese risotto with wrapped monkfish 186–7
mulligatawny soup 152–3
mushroom and two-grain risotto 126–7
paella 166–7
prawn gumbo 116–17
saffron and red pepper risotto 128–9
smoked haddock kedgeree 150–1
tomato risotto 63
risotto
butternut squash, with hazelnut butter 188–9
Milanese, with wrapped monkfish 186–7

mushroom and two-grain 126–7
saffron and red pepper 128–9
tomato 63
saffron and red pepper risotto 128–9
salad
broad bean and feta 44–5
calorie counter 231
chicken Caesar 156–7
couscous 94–5
deluxe fig and ham 38–9
exotic fruit 136–7
Greek pasta 100
grilled avocado, tomato and mozzarella 98–9
hot smoked salmon 42–3
panzanella 47
quinoa and halloumi 160–1
smoked mackerel superfood 96–7
sprouted bean and mango 46
throw-it-all-together 36–7
warm spiced salad Niçoise 158–9
white bean 101
salmon
and bulgur wheat pilau 112–13
hot smoked, salad 42–3
warm spiced salad Niçoise 158–9
salt 11
sardine
penne puttanesca 184
on toast 48–9
sauces, calorie counter 232
sausage
and gnocchi one-pan 110–11
Sunday brunch bake 84–5
Scotch broth 154–5
seafood, calorie counter 221
seeds, calorie counter 200–37
selenium 12
skewers, prawn & pineapple 60–1
slaw, apple 108–9
snacks, calorie counter 214–15
sodium 11, 12
sorbet, lemon 76
soufflés, chocolate 66–7
soup
beef pho 88–9
butternut squash, with cheesy toasts 34–5
calorie counter 233
chicken and dumpling 26–7
goulash 90–1
healthy fish chowder 30–1
mulligatawny 152–3
pea and ham 86–7
red lentil 92–3
Scotch broth 154–5
Vietnamese turkey noodle 28–9
spaghetti
courgette & goat's cheese 122–3
minestrone 32–3
Spanish omelette 146–7
spices, calorie counter 234

spinach
chicken tarragon sweet potatoes 106–7
poached egg with mushrooms 22–3
salmon and bulgur wheat pilau 112–13
sports drinks, calorie counter 203
spreads, calorie counter 219
Starbucks, calorie counter 218
starchy foods 10, 11
stew
beef and dumpling 182–3
Irish 174–5
Mexican chicken 102–3
strawberry
berry breakfast 17
three-ingredient ice-cream 77
toasted oats 80–1
stroke 10, 11
strudel, apple & blueberry 70–1
sugar 10
calorie counter 234
sugary foods/drinks 9, 11
summer pudding 68–9
Sunday brunch bake 84–5
superfood smoked mackerel salad 96–7
swede, beef and dumpling stew 182–3
sweet potato, chicken tarragon 106–7
sweetcorn, healthy fish chowder 30–1

tagine, chicken 52–3
takeaways, calorie counter 216–18
tenderstem broccoli
smoked mackerel superfood salad 96–7
zingy fish 56–7
Thai dressing 41
toast
beans on 82–3
cheesy toasts with butternut squash soup 34–5
French 21
sardines on 48–9
tomato
and basil sauce 62
cheesy chicken cobbler 104–5
chicken tagine 52–3
goat's cheese & onion slice 196–7
goulash soup 90–1
Greek pasta salad 100
griddled polenta ratatouille stack 194–5
harissa chicken & couscous salad 94–5
huevos rancheros 24–5
lamb spiced kebabs with crunchy coleslaw 170–1
lentil chilli 132–3
mozzarella & grilled avocado salad 98–9
mushroom and bean hotpot 134–5
panzanella salad 47

penne puttanesca 184
prawn gumbo 116–17
risotto 63
sardines on toast 48–9
spicy bean and potato 51
summer couscous 162
sunblush, and goat's cheese with pasta 185
Sunday brunch bake 84–5
turkey meatballs with barbecue sauce 168–9
veggie minestrone 32–3
vegetable frittata 64–5
warm spiced salad Niçoise 158–9
tortillas
beef fajitas 180–1
Cajun fish wraps 114–15
traffic light labelling 13
tropical fruit pots 14
turkey
calorie counter 226
meatballs, with barbecue sauce 168–9
noodle, Vietnamese soup 28–9

vegetables 11, 234–5
see also specific vegetables
vegetarian products, calorie counter 236–7
Vietnamese turkey noodle soup 28–9
vitamins 10, 12

weight loss, healthy 8, 9
wholegrains 11
wraps, Cajun fish 114–15

yogurt
apple slaw 108–9
calorie counter 211
creamy prawn and pea penne 120–1
crunchy coleslaw 170–1
toasted oats with berries 80–1

zinc 12